Beinn Eighe

The mountain above the wood

Beinn Eighe

The mountain above the wood

The story of the first fifty years
of Britain's first National Nature Reserve

J Laughton Johnston
and
Dick Balharry

First published in Great Britain in 2001 by

Birlinn Ltd
West Newington House
Newington Road
Edinburgh
EH9 1QS
www.birlinn.co.uk

Pencil and wash illustrations © John Busby

ISBN 1 84158 178 X **hbk**
      1 84158 193 3 **pbk**

British Library Cataloguing-in-Publication Data
A catalogue for this book is available on request from the British Library

Design by Christina Unwin

Printed and bound in Spain by Bookprint, S.L., Barcelona

Contents

Foreword *by Rhona Brankin*

National Nature Reserves have been the public face of our national system for the protection of our native wildlife, geology and natural landforms for the past 50 years. They hold a very special place in the Scottish psyche, being the very best of our characteristic natural places, be they mountain, forest, loch or coast. What they protect and manage though is not just a background to our lives, but the very weft through which our culture is woven. Who does not know lines from Robert Burns or Sorley MacLean, or passages from Robert Louis Stevenson or Iain Banks that extol the wild life or the shy life that is uniquely Scotland? Our native nature is as much a part of us as our art, song and literature.

But National Nature Reserves also protect and enhance those elements of our living environmental history that have become scarce or even rare through thousands of years of our management of the land. They are reservoirs of our natural resources from which we can learn and from which we can draw native seed to diversify and enhance the wider environment of Scotland.

Our National Nature Reserves therefore require to be looked after with great care. For fifty years now this task has been carried out by a dedicated group of scientists, naturalists and administrators, firstly as members of the Great Britain Nature Conservancy and latterly, in Scotland, as Scottish Natural Heritage. As Deputy Minister for Environment & Rural Development, I have the privilege of being responsible for the natural heritage of Scotland and Scottish Natural Heritage. I take this responsibility very seriously as our countryside, including National Nature Reserves, is a very important national resource upon which several of our key industries, such as tourism, agriculture and forestry depend. Today our National Nature Reserves and SNH itself play an increasingly important role in the environmental agenda and it heartens me to see this role embraced in the closing chapter of this book.

The responsibility for designation and management of National Nature Reserves and nature conservation in the wider environment in Scotland was fully devolved in 1991 with the formation of the Nature Conservancy Council for Scotland. The following year this body amalgamated with the Countryside Commission for Scotland to form Scottish Natural Heritage. One of the many repercussions of this amalgamation was a subtle change in the role and place of National Nature Reserves in the Scottish environment. They remain the pick of the very best of our native natural heritage, but have also taken on new purposes in relation to education, public access and enjoyment and the local community.

Originally, when Beinn Eighe was declared in 1951 the first of many National Nature Reserves (NNR) in Britain, their role was perceived by their founders to be that of open-air laboratories. Within their boundaries we would learn how to conserve and enhance our unique wildlife and landscape inheritance by the most natural means possible – ecological management. Perhaps also, we would then be in a position to apply this new expertise to the benefit of the wider environment of Scotland.

This book, celebrating the fiftieth birthday of Beinn Eighe NNR, tells the story of the first, and one of the most fascinating and extraordinary, of the 380 or so NNRs in Britain and Northern Ireland. It is a story of the vision of the founders of nature conservation and the painstaking trial and effort of the dedicated and pioneering ecologists and wardens who struggled to turn vision into action, which at Beinn Eighe was primarily the task of regenerating and expanding a unique outlier of Scotland's and Europe's Caledonian pinewood. It is the story of the changes in our attitudes to the natural environment and the development of the science of ecology and the techniques of nature conservation management that have occurred over the past fifty years: achieved by a long struggle of debate, pragmatism, trial and error. But such is how progress is achieved in all the sciences.

Beinn Eighe was a pioneering National Nature Reserve 50 years ago and still is today. NNRs, in addition to their primary task of the protection and enhancement of our natural heritage are now seen as important local resources. Beinn Eighe through its public facilities is an important link in the tourist economy of Wester Ross and the local community at Kinlochewe. Under the guidance of Scottish Natural Heritage this role has been strengthened and developed so that representatives of the local community now sit on the Reserve's management committee.

It is a pleasure and an honour to be in the position to write this foreword to the story of Britain and Scotland's very first National Nature Reserve, which has been such a beacon for the care and enjoyment of our unique natural heritage. Today, we should be immensely proud of Beinn Eighe, the many staff of the Nature Conservancy and Scottish Natural Heritage and the community of Kinlochewe, who have all contributed so much to its success over its first half-century.

I wish Beinn Eighe and all those associated with it a very happy anniversary and, as we say in Scotland, 'many more may you see'.

Rhona Brankin MSP

Foreword *by Chris Smith*

It was in 1965 that I first came to the Beinn Eighe National Nature Reserve. I was thirteen years old, had only once been to the Highlands before, and had put my name down for this fortnight's school 'project' with a mixture of excitement and trepidation. It was early May; the gorse was in full flower; there was still a dusting of snow on the mountain tops; and when we bundled ourselves off the train at Achnasheen we were bowled over by the enchanted landscape that started unfolding in front of us. The following two weeks were to change my life.

There must have been about twelve of us, all third-formers from George Watson's College in Edinburgh, and we were to spend the next fortnight staying in Anancaun, with some side-nights off at the Scottish Mountaineering Club Hut in Glen Torridon. We climbed the mountains. We walked the glens. We measured the growth of new seedlings in the pinewoods. We made maps of the way the forest was regenerating. We played football. We learned about the flora and fauna. And we fell in love with the whole Torridon area.

I have been back time and again since. Indeed, when I was a University student I spent three summers as resident volunteer warden at Craig Youth Hostel on the shores of Loch Torridon beyond Diabaig. And those high ridges of the Torridon hills, steep and jagged and complex, have drawn me back many times. During that May fortnight in 1965 I climbed my first Munro: Beinn Liath Mhor, on the south side of Glen Torridon. I remember it was grey and wet and the cloud was low down and like many a mountain since I couldn't see a thing from the summit. But it was place of wildness and freedom, and getting there was hard and exhilarating, and I thought then and there that this was something to be done again and again. And then the following day we climbed Liathach in the most glorious sunshine with half the western seaboard spread around us, and I knew that I was right. Twenty-four years later I completed all the Munros.

The greatest gift that fortnight at the Beinn Eighe reserve gave me was the love of the mountains and the wilderness. But it taught me, too, about the delicacy of the relationship between humankind and the natural world. It showed us about the fragility of the environment, and about the things we can now do to try and put right the damage of the centuries. It showed us how regeneration, slow and painful though it may be, can indeed happen. And that of course is the lesson of fifty years of dedicated work at Beinn Eighe, chronicled in this excellent book by Laughton Johnston and Dick Balharry. They have set out the excitements of the original foundation of the reserve, the debates over fending and replanting and ploughing and seeding, the ups and downs of deer management strategies, and the inspiration that has been given to generations of visitors. The story turns out to be - though rooted in one particular place - the history of conservation, land management and ecology for half a century in Scotland. And it has profound lessons to teach us.

Dick Balharry was the Warden at Anancaun when I first came there thirty-six years ago. This book is a testament to his contribution, and that of many others, to a very special place. Above all, it is a tribute to the enduring beauty of the Beinn Eighe National Nature Reserve itself.

Rt. Hon. Chris Smith MP
2001

Preface

In writing this book we have had access to all the existing Reserve files and have interviewed thirty-five individuals who have been involved with Beinn Eighe, before and since its establishment, covering the period from 1947 to 2001. Fortunately, several of the original and critical players in the story are still alive and well and we were able to piece together the earliest events in London, Edinburgh and Kinlochewe.

All in all, we were given and found, far more material than we could possibly use and have been forced to make very difficult choices as to what to use and what to discard. We apologise if we have left out some favourite anecdotes, but we hope those involved will agree that we have kept the gist of the story. Inevitably, those years of discussion, experiment and change, notably the early years, take up more space than those years of steady progress under an agreed management plan. Even though those latter years are not given as much space in this book, they were just as important as any others in contributing towards the final achievement of the original aims of the Reserve.

We are very grateful for all the help and support we have had from all those we have interviewed and we apologise to those whom we have missed. We would like to thank Scottish Natural Heritage for the provision of the majority of the photographs and the preparation of all the maps and diagrams. We would also like to thank others who have contributed photographs and those who read and commented on the text. We are particularly grateful to Donald McVean and Tim Clifford for permission to use their tree graphs of age, and to Roy Wentworth for checking the spelling and English meaning of the Gaelic names. We would also like to acknowledge the very helpful comments and editing of John Walters and Wendy Simpson. Finally, our thanks to David Miller and the staff at the Beinn Eighe office for putting up with all our intrusions and questions.

JLJ & DB

A' Bheinn air Chall

Tha bheinn ag éirigh os cionn coille,
air chall anns a' choille th' air chall,
Is bhristeadh sinn air clàr ar gréine
On a tha na speuran teann.

Air chall ann an aomadh na coille
iomhaighean iomadhthach ar spéis.

Somhairlie MacGill-Eain

The Lost Mountain

The Mountain rises above the wood,
lost in the wood that is lost,
and we have been broken on the board of our sun
since the skies are tight.

Lost in the decline of the wood
the many-coloured images of our aspiration.

Sorley MacLean

1 The mountain

'At that time dense and extensive woods along the south shore of Loch Maree, consisting of pine, birch, oak, aspen, elm and holly, described as some of the best woods in the West of Scotland...'

Timothy Pont, 1600 (from Steven & Carlisle, 1959)

Beginnings

Place has no meaning until it is named, for it is through a name that we come to visualise and empathise with place, even when we may never have seen that place. This is particularly true of the Gaelic names in this story of one of the remoter parts of Britain. For those of us who do not know the language, we need those names translated into English and then – immediately and magically – we find ourselves relating to the landscape and its history. The remnant of the ancient Caledonian pine forests at Beinn Eighe is Coille na Glas Leitir or 'wood of the grey slope'; it is called that because of the presence of a woodland on the otherwise bare, grey flanks of a mountain known as Beinn Eighe or 'file- or saw-toothed mountain', after its long, sharp and triangular ridge. It is this relatively tiny remnant of ancient pinewood, on the farthest western margin of the European-wide Scots pine forests that led to the site being purchased in 1951 by the Government's recently formed Nature Conservancy and declared a National Nature Reserve.

That simple act of purchase was the official birth of nature conservation: the protection and management of native wildlife in the British Isles. The nature conservation movement has now grown to take a central place in our care and enjoyment of the land – not only of wild land, but of farmland, croftland and forest.

When Beinn Eighe was declared Britain's first National Nature Reserve (NNR), to many readers of The Times, in which the official notice appeared on 24 November 1951, it could only have meant a mountain somewhere in Scotland. To the majority of Scots it was simply somewhere in the Highlands. Only a few climbers and local people knew it as the mountain near the village of Kinlochewe, in Wester Ross, on the western coast of the North-West Highlands. Very few would have known the purpose of a National Nature Reserve.

The north-west coast of Scotland is like a giant jigsaw puzzle without its edge pieces, fretted by long freshwater and sea lochs that wind into its mountains. Constant exposure to the Atlantic Ocean, has resulted in the sea's exploitation of lines of weakness running in from the coast. More recently, relatively speaking,

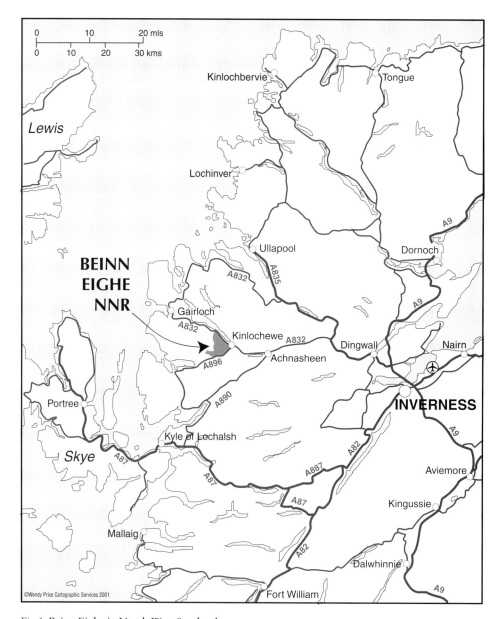

Fig 1 **Beinn Eighe in North-West Scotland.**

tongues of ice from glaciers have also exploited these weaknesses, but from the opposite direction. Wester Ross is typical of this pattern. Here the sea has intruded to the base of a conglomeration of mountains, many over 1000 m, that stand as bastions against the weather systems that track in from the Atlantic, earning an enormous annual rainfall for their trouble. Beinn Eighe itself and the mountains of Torridon of which it is part, an area some 30 km by 15 km, bordered by the saltwaters of Loch Torridon to the south and the freshwaters of Loch Maree to the north, is just one piece of the puzzle. Beyond their shores for over 100 km in either direction lie dozens of other similar pieces, protruded and indented that inflict a long, slow, but entertaining journey for the traveller.

This is one of the least hospitable and yet most beautiful parts of Scotland and the most rugged of the Highlands. It is a place where people, plants and animals have struggled to survive. The mountains do not have the comparatively gentle curves and dry soils of the Cairngorms to the east or the green lushness of the mountains of Kintail to the south. Here, they are often steep-sided and their rock bones of ancient Cambrian Quartzite and Torridonian Sandstone lie exposed, unremittingly hard and often wet. In general appearance it is a barren and desolate landscape, described by Scotland's adopted naturalist of the mid-twentieth century, Frank Fraser Darling, as a 'largely devastated terrain'. Because of its physical nature and its climate it is a difficult country in which to travel, remote as it is, from the centres of population. With a few notable exceptions very few travellers and writers of the eighteenth and nineteenth centuries visited or popularised it, as happened with the Trossachs, the Cairngorms, Skye and the Western Isles. The Scottish cartographer, Timothy Pont, passed by on his travels in the late sixteenth century. Pennant traversed Loch Maree in 1772 on his tour of the Highlands, landing on Isle Maree and commenting briefly on its beautiful grove of trees. One hundred years later, in 1877, Queen Victoria passed along the shore en route to the Loch Maree Hotel and rewarded the scene a paragraph or two in her Highland Journal. It is really only since the 1940s through improved roads and a car-owning population that the area has become better known.

That is, those parts of the country visible from the few roads that snake through the glens, along rivers and lochsides and around the coast. For there are vast areas of mountain terrain, tens of square kilometres in extent that are inaccessible except on foot. Not for nothing is the area known to climbers and walkers as the 'great wilderness'. Large private estates traditionally have rarely welcomed walkers, so that only the privileged and the intrepid have explored the land surrounding Beinn Eighe. For example, to the north lies the private estate of Letterewe – eight times the area of the first National Nature Reserve. Today Beinn Eighe is in public hands, while neighbouring Torridon is in the hands of The National Trust for Scotland and therefore both are unrestricted to visitors. Soon, perhaps, the Scottish Land Reform Bill will make accessible to the public virtually all land. In the 1950s, however, Wester Ross was not an easy or receptive place in which to sow the radical seed of nature conservation management and public enjoyment of the countryside.

The two approaches to Kinlochewe by road for the visitor from the south are via Shieldaig and Torridon or via Achnasheen from Inverness. The former route presents a grand view of the adjacent Torridon mountains from the south shore of Loch Torridon, but much of the great ridge of Beinn Eighe is obscured. It is only when one has passed by the mighty Liathach in Glen Torridon that the southern

Walkers climbing Beinn Eighe
from the Coire an Laoigh path
with Torridon
in the background.
Photo: J. MacPherson / SNH

flanks of Beinn Eighe with their great, white quartzite screes begin to show themselves. A better view of Beinn Eighe, and the one that remains in the memory of so many visitors, is that to be seen on the latter route. First, at Achnasheen, after driving through relatively low and rounded hills there is suddenly a distant view beyond those hills of a rugged skyline to the west, comprising the sharp pyramidal peaks of Liathach and the whole imposing length of the jagged ridge of Beinn Eighe. It is a tantalising view because as the road passes Achnasheen and begins the climb over to Glen Docherty the mountains become hidden. From the top of Glen Docherty, just where the road begins its winding descent to the village of Kinlochewe, there is an impressive view north-west towards the coast at Poolewe, overlooking a 20-km glen in which lies Loch Maree (named after the Irish monk, Maelrubha). It is only at Kinlochewe itself that Beinn Eighe reappears, but now the traveller is too close to see the mountain for its foothills. The road from Kinlochewe then branches, southwest to Torridon or straight on along the Beinn Eighe side of Loch Maree towards Gairloch. Two hundred years ago the route along the north side of the loch under the towering bulk of Slioch was traditionally taken by drovers and their cattle from the Western Isles on their annual journey to the markets in the east.

Beinn Eighe is a mountain mass within a sea of mountains and is best viewed only after a hard climb, from the heights of those surrounding mountains. Only then can one truly appreciate the scale of its 8-km, sweeping ridge, its stark barrenness, deep corries and the wide fans of eroded quartzite that pour off its ridge. The view from any angle of these magnificent mountains, however, raises the same questions: how and when did they form, how were they shaped, why are they so barren, why is the forest so discontinuous along the lower slopes and along the shores of Loch Maree? And for how long have people made a living from this land, which, apart from the floor of the glen, is so inhospitable?

Moreover, how did Coille na Glas Leitir, that remote pinewood remnant, become the centre of attention for the newly formed Nature Conservancy, the national press, naturalists and conservationists throughout Britain in 1951? Why has the management of this relatively small area, over a period of fifty years, remained a subject of fascination and heated discussion among naturalists and foresters, and what lay behind its many changes of management over the years? How did this remote corner of land become the test-bed for nature conservation management and countryside interpretation in Britain, leading the field in many cases and setting examples in others that were to be followed all over the country?

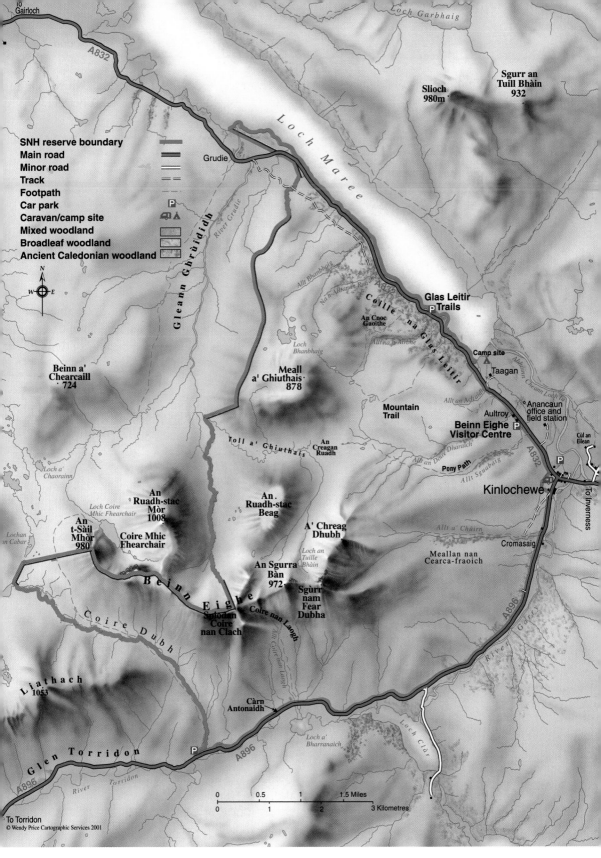

Fig 2 Base map of Beinn Eighe with place-names.

To find the answers to those questions we will look first at both the forces of nature and the less dramatic but equally important forces of human endeavour, that have shaped the land and the living mantle of Wester Ross and Beinn Eighe. In the next chapter we will turn our attention to the origins of the Nature Conservancy and the purchase of Beinn Eighe. Thereafter, we will examine the ground-breaking and extraordinary developments in nature conservation and visitor management at the Reserve and the struggles and hopes of the people who pioneered the art of native woodland restoration and those who served on the Reserve from its declaration in 1951 to the present.

The shaping of Beinn Eighe

A vivid description of the geology of Beinn Eighe is provided by W. H. Murray in *The Compaanion Guide to the West Highlands of Scotland* (1968):

> You could not have a better introduction to Torridon mountains than the approach to Kinlochewe – halt by the roadside at Loch Clair. To the right of the road are two of the finest mountain ranges of Scotland – Beinn Eighe and Liathach. Beinn Eighe means in Gaelic 'The File' and truly its seven tops on its seven-mile ridge seem not unlike a file. Both mountains are largely red sandstone but Beinn Eighe's four eastern tops are entirely of Cambrian quartzite – giving an aspect of white sterility, yet enhancing the grace of the sharp summit ridge, swinging from peak to peak. Liathach means 'The Grey One' – it, too, has seven tops, four of them quartzite. A ridge of five miles links them, but from Loch Clair one has eyes for only one. It is the soaring peak of the North; a mountain of sombre sandstone, it springs to an arrowhead of white quartzite, 3000 ft above the road.

To the geologist the rocks of Beinn Eighe tell an incredible story. The reddish-coloured rock that makes up most of the mountain and its neighbours is Torridonian Sandstone, a rock that occurs as a broad band down the north-west coast of Scotland. This was originally laid down as sediment of great depth by large river systems around 1000 million years ago on top of an even more ancient Lewisian surface. These sediments hardened into rock and then went through hundreds of millions of years of compaction and erosion.

Around 550 million years ago more sediments began to be deposited on top of the Torridonian Sandstones. These became the Cambrian rocks and by their composition and texture geologists can tell that parts of them were laid down in a shallow marine situation. These are quartzites and are the white and shattered rocks that now cap Beinn Eighe like icing on the Torridonian Sandstone cake. Other parts of the Cambrian rocks were laid down in deeper seawater and they contain the oldest known marine fossils in Britain. On Beinn Eighe these rocks are known as the Fucoid Beds and they occur especially within Meall a' Ghiuthais (*hill of the pines*). Some of these Cambrian rocks are lime-rich from the ancient shellfish deposits and in a few areas have a very visible effect on the composition of Beinn Eighe's plants.

At this time of the deposition of the Cambrian rocks the future countries of Scotland and England stood on different continents separated by an ocean. The fossils of the Fucoid Beds are the actual proof of this ocean and therefore a key

The triple buttresses of the mighty Coire Mhic Fhearchair.
Photo: R. Balharry

The pink flowers
of the dwarf shrub
mountain azalea.
Photo: D. Miller

feature in the evolutionary story of the British Isles. It is a curious coincidence that the boundary between these continents is not too far away from the present political boundary between the countries!

Today on the Beinn Eighe Mountain Trail, many of these features are quite apparent, for example at Trumpet Rock the remains of tubes within which lived Cambrian worms are plainly visible, while the visual effect of the lime-rich Cambrian rocks can be seen in the presence of 'greens' – sweet grasses among the brown heaths that attract the grazing deer. If one looks across Loch Maree to Slioch from high up on the Trail, all that remains of the Torridonian Sandstone after its millions of years of erosion – the top 800 metres – can plainly be distinguished sitting on the Lewisian base.

Not long after the laying down of the Cambrian rocks, geologically speaking, some 430 million years ago, the continents on which stood Scotland and England collided. One of the results of that enormous collision was the upthrust of the

Prostrate juniper
clinging to rocks.
Photo: D. Miller

Herbertus borealis,
a liverwort
occurring otherwise
only in Norway.
Photo: D. Miller

Highlands. Another was a great shearing of rocks along a 160-km line that runs from Loch Eriboll on the north coast all the way down to the south end of the Isle of Skye, known to geologists as the Moine Thrust. This event forced wedges of older rocks onto the top of younger rocks. Evidence for this is an outlier of older Torridonian rock sitting on the top of the younger Cambrian rocks of Meall a' Ghiuthais.

After these gigantic geological upheavals there followed another immense period of attrition by river and aerial erosion and then a very much shorter period, of glaciation. During this last period an enormous covering of ice carved the finer features of Beinn Eighe as we see them today – the sharp ridge for example and the magnificent Coire Mhic Fhearchair (*corrie of the son of Farquhar*) with its great triple buttresses. It also smoothed the sides of an ancient river bed, that itself had exploited an offshoot of the Moine Thrust, to form the glen in which now lies Loch Maree and it created many smaller sculptures, bowls and hillocks that can be seen all around the flanks of the mountain.

The northern emerald,
a dragonfly
in a sheltered bog.
Photo: D. Miller

As the ice departed, still freezing temperatures then shattered the summit quartzite rocks that spill today so dangerously down Beinn Eighe's steep slopes. Finally, as the icy-cold climate came to an end some 12,000 years ago and the climate ameliorated, the growth of the living mantle began with colonisation by lichens and mosses, the formation of soils and the subsequent arrival of arctic-alpine and tundra plants. This part of Scotland, near the west coast, then came under the influence of milder Atlantic weather and around 8500 years ago a pine forest dominated by Scots pine became established ahead of its counterpart in the Central Highlands. We will return to the origin of these trees in a later chapter, when the evidence for their very early arrival was discovered and caused a reversal of many years of effort on the National Nature Reserve.

As the climate continued to improve, those pioneering plants and animals, adapted to cold and unstable conditions, became isolated at higher altitudes, where the climate remains harsh to this day. On Beinn Eighe many arctic-alpine and mountain plants can still be found on the tiny lime-rich beds, or on the seepage areas below them. The soils derived from the hard Torridonian Sandstones and the quartzites that predominate, however, are relatively poor and they lost much of their limited reservoir of plant-important minerals as the climate became milder and wetter.

The hard-won view from the desolate summit of Beinn Eighe at its highest point on Ruadh Stac Mór is breathtaking: that is, when it is not covered in cloud and beaten by wind and rain. On a clear day all around are mountains and shadows of mountains, shimmering lochs and lochans and to the west the Atlantic and the hills of Harris, upward of 100 km away. To the immediate south-west are the great peaks of Liathach and the other Torridon mountains and beyond them the Red and Black Cuillins of Skye. To the south are Beinn Damh and the distant green mountains of Kintail. To the north, across the blue cleft of Loch Maree, Slioch towers before a mass of peaks, among which An Teallach at 1060 m and even Ben Mór Assynt at more than 70 km away, can be made out. To the east beyond Kinlochewe, moulded on a gentler scale, are the Fannich Hills and Ben Wyvis. However, while the ridge, peaks and corries of Beinn Eighe have always drawn climbers, the mountain is not for the inexperienced.

Beinn Eighe's wildlife

Superlatives also abound in the description of the individual features of Beinn Eighe's wildlife, such as its Caledonian pinewood and many rare and nationally scarce plants and animals. However, its nature conservation value lies as much in the altitudinal range of its plant communities, stretching from a mild and damp oceanic climate to the fierce and freezing arctic of the summits, as in one or two exceptional communities. Very few of the many National Nature Reserves (NNR) today have this complement of vegetation from sea level to 1000 m. On the ridges and summits, plant cover consists only of a thin and ragged carpet of moss with tiny mountain sedges, rushes and uncommon arctic-alpine flowers, such as the delicate pink pincushion of moss campion. Everywhere there are the signs of wind and frost – plants clinging to the shelter of stones and loose fragments of rock and the characteristic polygonal pattern of frost heave in the soil.

On the south side it is a steep and continuous descent from the ridge, but on the north side, avoiding the loose and dangerous quartzite screes and the almost vertically sided corries, half-way down there is a plateau at around 500 m lying between the summit ridge and the lower slopes that fall away to Loch Maree. This apparently barren scene is one of the largest areas of quartzite plateau in Britain. Plant cover is very sparse, with patches of ground-hugging shrubs such as heather, crowberry, alpine bearberry and the occasional mountain azalea with its tiny pink and red flowers. Extraordinarily, this high-level plateau is also home to one of the most extensive British populations of the sharp-leaved, prostrate juniper, as well as *Herbertus borealis*, a bright orange leafy liverwort, otherwise known in the world only from three sites in Norway. This is the country of our northern birds such as ptarmigan, dotterel and snow bunting, also of mountain hare and the summer home of red deer. Here, dragonflies hover over crystal-clear lochans and palmate newts lie doggo in the shallows. The terrain and its wildlife at this altitude mirror that of the arctic tundra more than 1500 km to the north.

Leaving the plateau and descending steeply to around 300 m above Loch Maree the low shrubby ground cover gradually becomes continuous. This is the altitudinal limit for trees on Beinn Eighe, where small rowans cling to the sides of crags outwith the reach of deer and hare. But as the descent enters the very top of one of the narrow ravines, birch, aspen, holly and Scots pine become common and one quickly enters the upper part of the pine forest. In this more sheltered terrain and milder climate shrubs grow increasingly taller and as the slope flattens, mires of bog moss occur with scented bog myrtle. Lower down still, towards the shores of Loch Maree, oak appear with alder and occasional bushes of upright juniper, a plant more common in the pinewoods to the east. Under a closing woodland canopy, wildlife diversity increases overhead with redstart, tits and the Scottish crossbill, while hidden in the undergrowth small mammals such as voles and mice scurry about unseen. There are rare creatures too, though alas we are lucky even to see their tracks, such as the pine marten and wildcat. This is the pine woodland proper, the oceanic woodland of north-west Scotland, where very high rainfall and humidity has resulted in the richest community of liverworts and mosses of any woodland in Britain, quite unlike the drier pinewood forests of the Cairngorms. Varied as they are from west to east, the Scottish pinewoods are actually only the western limit of a vastly more heterogeneous coniferous boreal forest that stretches around the world from Europe to Asia and across North America.

Until the 1960s very few of us were familiar with native Scots pinewood, since there is very little of it left in Wester Ross, or even Scotland as a whole (see Fig 3). But in that decade the Nature Conservancy constructed one of the very first nature trails in Britain through Coille na Glas Leitir. Shortly after, a second circular trail was hewn out of the steep slope up to the high-level plateau. Today, thanks to colourful and entertaining leaflets, you can walk the Woodland and Mountain Trails and explore it for yourself.

So was there always very little tree cover? Emphatically, no: around 6000 years ago, when it was drier and warmer than it is now, the landscape to about 300 m in Wester Ross had a great deal more tree cover. Thereafter, around 4000 years ago, the climate, especially in the north and west, deteriorated, becoming cooler and wetter. The result was deterioration in the productivity of the soil, waterlogging and the onset of the formation of peat and its inexorable spread. In effect, many of the soils could no longer support trees and this combined with more recent relentless human management prevented tree regeneration, leading to the familiar and almost treeless landscape we see today: a landscape, however, that is well below its productive potential.

The human impact

The story of people in Wester Ross begins around the time of the first pinewoods. The earliest were the hunter-gatherers whose exploitation of their environment was on the whole sustainable. Then there were the farmers who, through their pastoral and arable management, gradually cleared the forests and hindered their regrowth. Through 100 generations the forests became woods, became copses until there were very few left, usually on land unsuitable for crops or awkward for grazing. In historical times the people who lived in North-West Scotland were members of the Pictish tribes that occupied most of the country north of the Forth/Clyde valley. Known to the Romans as the Cantae, they later, for several centuries after AD 800, came under the rule of the Vikings who had plundered and then taken the Western and Northern Isles. Thereafter, following the Scots defeat of the Norse, from 1300 at least, the land of the north-west and its people, fell under the sway of the MacLeods and the MacKenzies of Kintail, Scots incomers from the south-west. The most infamous and certainly most colourful of the MacKenzies was Black Murdo of the Cave. In the 1350s he slew the followers of Leod Mac Gilleandreis, who had taken his family's lands at Kinlochewe, then decapitated them and threw their heads into the Abhainn Cheann Loch Iù *(river of Kinlochewe)*. Eventually these bloody, severed heads came aground downstream, gathering at a shallow point in the river known today as Anancaun (Àth nan Ceann *ford of the heads)*. Most of the region's Gaelic names have emerged from this era, although many others may be derived from the earlier Norse period, such as the name Beinn Eighe itself, and some may even have come down from the area's original inhabitants. Incidentally, Anancaun is now the base for the Beinn Eighe NNR and local SNH staff.

Up to the beginning of the seventeenth century the MacKenzies held Kinlochewe and the MacLeods held Gairloch, but subsequently the MacKenzies

Red deer and woodland are natural partners.
Photo: J. MacPherson / SNH

became the proprietors of all the land in the Beinn Eighe area. This may have been a remote area of Scotland but it was no backwater. In the early seventeenth century occurred the first systematic exploitation of the woodlands of the area, with the establishment of some of the very earliest ironworks in Scotland in 1607. This occurred at Furnace in Letterewe, on the north side of Loch Maree opposite Beinn Eighe, as well as at several other sites in the area. There is little doubt that from earliest times people had made direct use of these forests and their timber, both pine and broadleaves, but the ironworks led to wholesale felling of mainly oak and birch for charcoal. The ironworks lasted for sixty years until the timber was all but exhausted, manufacturing wrought iron and pig iron, and cast-iron cannons among other products, for the whole of Scotland. There must have been extensive woodlands all around Loch Maree and especially on the north side, where the main ironworks were situated, to have supported the industry for so long. J. H. Dixon (*Gairloch and Guide to Loch Maree*, 1886) noted that the annual consumption of each furnace was equivalent to 120 acres of wood! Although the timber of broadleaves was preferred, it is probable that once they were becoming scarce there would have been exploitation of the pinewood also. Irish foresters also operated right up the west coast of Scotland as far as Loch Maree at this time, seeking bark for tanning, having used up most of their own sources and they too might have exploited pinewood timber. There is also evidence that woodland was cleared in the seventeenth century to destroy the habitat of the wolf, long gone by then from farther south in Britain.

From the earliest farmers right up to the nineteenth century and the end of the Highland clan culture, agricultural use of Beinn Eighe and its lower slopes was for pasturing domestic stock that consisted mainly of black cattle and a few sheep and goats. After the Highland Clearances in the late eighteenth and early nineteenth centuries, the intensity of grazing increased with the introduction of large flocks of more modern breeds of sheep from the south and the removal of cattle from the hill and sometimes people from the glens. Beinn Eighe itself, however, carried little sheep, except for a very limited area of common grazings attached to Kinlochewe. It was far more important as part of the Kinlochewe Deer Forest. The impact of the Clearances on Kinlochewe was therefore much less than elsewhere in the Highlands.

Along with the introduction of deer-stalking and grouse-shooting in the eighteenth and nineteenth centuries came a concomitant great increase in the population of red deer and also regular muirburn. Burning the heather was designed to burn off the old unpalatable twiggy shoots and promote new and delicate growth for sheep and grouse. These developments led to ever-increasing pressure of grazing and burning on the hill, principally below the 300 m contour that must have caused the transformation of much moorland to grassland and prevented any regeneration of the remaining woodlands. The total impact on the woodlands, of the iron and tanning industries and subsequent sporting and grazing management was devastating. It is difficult now for us to imagine what the countryside around Loch Maree must have looked like prior to these events, but luckily, there is a description of the woodland by Timothy Pont, the great Scottish perambulator and cartographer of the late sixteenth century: 'in sum places with fair and beautiful fyrrs [Scots pine] of 60, 70, 80 foot of good and serviceable timmer for masts and raes [sail yards], in other places ar great plentie of excellent great oakes, whaer may be sawin out planks of 4 sumtyms [5 foot] broad'. A somewhat different place even such a short time ago.

Steven and Carlisle (1959) have explained that these pinewoods were 'certainly more extensive in early historical times, for example they probably stretched from Loch Maree towards Achnashellach, while the southern shores of Upper Loch Torridon may have been partly pine'. In the Blaeu Atlas of 1654, based on Pont's descriptions and therefore prior to the systematic exploitation of the Loch Maree woodlands, the boundary of Coille na Glas Leitir is already that which was found just before the Second World War and its final exploitation. It may well be therefore that Coille na Glas Leitir itself was not exploited to any great extent at that time: the ironworks were, of course, on the other side of Loch Maree.

One of the very many questions modern woodland ecologists would have liked to have asked Pont is: were the pine woodlands open in nature like the remnant we see today at Coille na Glas Leitir and the Shieldaig pinewoods on the south side of Loch Torridon, or were they more like the dense, even-aged native coniferous forests of Norway? Pont's description of 'fyrrs of 60, 70, 80 foot of good and serviceable timmer for masts' hints at the latter, in at least 'sum places'. This is not merely academic curiosity, but one that became very important for the Conservancy staff in the 1970s when their pioneering efforts in the restoration of Coille na Glas Leitir ran up against this conundrum.

Coille na Glas Leitir

The history of the National Nature Reserve at Beinn Eighe is as much the history of the management and restoration of Coille na Glas Leitir since 1951, as any of the other innovative projects that have made Beinn Eighe so well known to conservationists, naturalists, foresters, climbers and visitors. So why was the purchase and restoration of Coille na Glas Leitir so important and why should we be so grateful that it was bought? At the time and for most people it was simply a case of protecting one of the last pieces of ancient pinewood in the far north-west for future study. No one had any firm ideas about how it was to be protected, or if anything else needed to be done to ensure its future, apart from declaring it a Reserve. We did not generally realise then just how important such places would prove to be. Luckily, there were one or two visionaries who did have an inkling. We will meet these people in this story and will return to their vision and those of later conservationists at the very end, when the world about the wood and the wood itself had undergone enormous changes.

The oldest trees of Coille na Glas Leitir are some 350 years of age and from the evidence of ancient burnt stumps and a charcoal layer that can still be seen in the peat, it appears that there must have been a great fire that destroyed the majority of these older trees some 300 years ago. Was it a natural event or man-made? We will probably never know. Most of the mature trees that exist today therefore sprang from their forebear's ashes. The very oldest trees – mere saplings when Scotland's last independent Parliament met in 1707 and granny trees by 1999 on the opening of Scotland's new devolved Parliament – are therefore both the source of all the regenerating trees we can see around them today and a direct link to the very first pines that grew here, perhaps only 8000 years ago. If pine trees at Beinn Eighe can live and set viable seed up to an age of 350 years, which is probably a conservative estimate, some of the pine trees have a lineage of only twenty-five generations since the first tree grew here.

There is further evidence that the penultimate exploitation of the pinewood may have been 150 years ago, not long after the potato famines that caused such hardship in the West of Scotland and Ireland. This was a time when people were forced to work on the construction of the 'destitution' roads – the very roads we now travel on to Beinn Eighe as visitors and tourists – to obtain food for themselves and their families. The late Farquhar MacDonald of Kinlochewe, a stalker on Beinn Eighe, who showed the Conservancy's first Scottish Director, John Berry, around Beinn Eighe on his initial visit in 1951, knew a man who had taken part in 1850 in clearing the Beinn Eighe ravine woods of Allt a' Chùirn (*burn of the cairn*) and Allt an Doire Dharaich (*burn of the hollow of the oaks*), both of which were formerly larger and perhaps contiguous patches of woodland. Timber taken from the latter ravine was probably used at that time in the construction of the lodge on the neighbouring Coulin estate.

The last felling in the pinewood, less than ten years before Beinn Eighe became a Nature Reserve, took place during the Second World War. The Ministry of Supply is said to have paid £4200 for the timber, with the proviso that only two-thirds of the trees should be felled. The Pioneer Corps – lumberjacks brought in from Newfoundland and British Honduras – carried out the work. Similar events took place at several other pinewoods in Scotland, for example at Mar Lodge Estate. Mrs Diana Greig, the last private owner of Coille na Glas Leitir, recalls being told that the lumberjacks felled nearly all the largest trees from two relatively accessible areas near the road, irrespective of whether or not the trees cut were the best for timber or reasonably easy to extract, leaving only some for amenity reasons near the road. Many cut trees were left, not just lying where they fell, but also stacked for removal and never taken out.

As far as the history of Coille na Glas Leitir over the last hundred years is known, it appears to have been used mainly as part of the Kinlochewe Deer Forest, giving winter shelter to stags in a landscape otherwise devoid of anything offering respite from that season's driving rain, sleet and snow. Until 1919, it was part of the land of the MacKenzies of Gairloch, today represented by John MacKenzie of Flowerdale. In 1920 the MacKenzies sold it to a Mr Hickman who sold it on to Mrs Greig in 1945. In his later years Hickman let the stag stalking and concentrated on grouse. There may well have been muirburn then that would have destroyed any natural regeneration on the periphery of the wood. Otherwise the only recorded burning was carried out after felling in the mid 1940s. According to Mrs Greig's keeper, Alistair Mackay, the size of the bogwood did not alter in his time. The part that is birch wood, he said, has always been birch and its grass floor has given good feeding for the deer.

Today, Coille na Glas Leitir, including the Loch Maree islands, is one of only five remaining pinewoods in Wester Ross out of a forest that once must have covered almost all the well-drained low ground. The others are Shieldaig, 20 km distant on the south side of Loch Torridon; Coulin, less than 5 km to the south-east; Achnashellach, another 5 km beyond the last; and a tiny fragment on the southern slopes of An Teallach 15 km to the north. All are relatively near each other and are described by Steven and Carlisle as in an area '… with a marked oceanic climate and high rainfall … [where] … Scots pine … often shows poor growth and tends to lose its needles after one or two years, hence it is of interest that the native pine has not only survived but has remained healthy through successful regeneration.' The inference here, in 1959, is that the trees of these pinewoods must be particularly adapted to the climate north-west Scotland, a point of great significance in the later management of Coille na Glas Leitir.

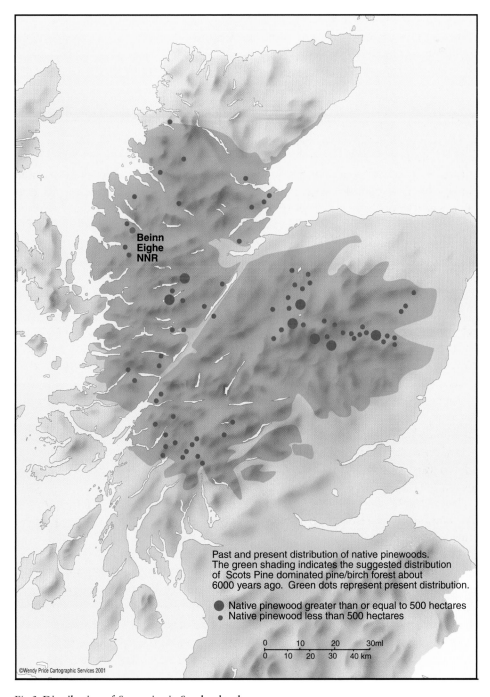

Past and present distribution of native pinewoods.
The green shading indicates the suggested distribution
of Scots Pine dominated pine/birch forest about
6000 years ago. Green dots represent present distribution.

● Native pinewood greater than or equal to 500 hectares
• Native pinewood less than 500 hectares

0   10   20   30ml
0   10   20   30   40 km

Beinn
Eighe
NNR

©Wendy Price Cartographic Services 2001

Fig 3 **Distribution of Scots pine in Scotland today.**

Happenstance is a wonderful thing. Just prior to the Second World War an English botanist and ecologist happened to visit the area and stumble across Coille na Glas Leitir. He was Sir Arthur Tansley, later Chairman of the Government Committee that oversaw the setting up of the Nature Conservancy. He described it thus: 'The pine forest on the south-western shore of Loch Maree towards the south-eastern end of the loch, and extending up a steep valley and adjoining slopes to the 1000 foot (300 m) contour, is one of the few native Highland pinewoods that is still freely regenerating.' Of the two people, the other being John Berry, who could legitimately claim to have played the most critical roles in the early purchase and protection of Coille na Glas Leitir as part of the very first National Nature Reserve in Britain, Tansley is the one who first plotted the area on the conservation map.

The 'barren' plateau
around 500m
below Meall a' Ghiuthais.
Photo: SNH

2 Birth of a Nature Reserve 1941–51

'... the pioneers of nature conservation had been trying for three years to pull out of the air what conservation was and how to make ecology become real. Suddenly, out of the blue, we were offered a wonderful tract of primeval woodland and mountain at Beinn Eighe. We had no idea what to do with it, but we could not refuse the offer. So we found ourselves learning the hard way what a National Nature Reserve was and how to manage it.'

E. M. Nicholson, 'The President's Message to the '49 Club', Beinn Eighe, 2000

Birth of the Nature Conservancy

The Second World War proved to be the catalyst for both the last exploitation of Coille na Glas Leitir's timber and, by coincidence, the impetus for the first steps in its regeneration. In the dark days of that period of British history a few far-sighted people were already looking ahead to the need for post-war planning. Through their influence the wartime coalition Government established a Ministry of Reconstruction, one of whose areas of concern became the future of the countryside, protection for wildlife, its study and its availability for enjoyment by a weary population that needed to rekindle a healthy and forward-looking spirit. In 1941 the Society for the Promotion of Nature Reserves, to which some of those people belonged, held a conference and issued a memorandum, one recommendation of which was 'that an official body should be appointed to consider proposals for nature preservation.' That conference then appointed a Nature Reserves Investigation Committee in June 1942 and it was the report of this committee that formed the building blocks of the report of the Government's own Wildlife Conservation Special Committee (WLCSC) in 1947. This latter report is still known to professional conservationists by its original official label: Command 7122. In it the committee recommended the creation of forty-seven Nature Reserves.

National Parks were dealt with by a second Government committee that took forward the landscape conservation and public access aspects of the countryside, which led to the creation of National Parks in England. In its turn, the WLCSC took forward issues of nature conservation that brought into being Nature Reserves throughout Britain. While it could be said that the former looked at the more obvious aspects of public enjoyment of the countryside and the preservation of the rural idyll, the latter was more evidently concerned with the gaining of scientific knowledge of the countryside and its application, not only for the purposes of the conservation of nature, but also for the benefit of other countryside users, such as agriculture and forestry. Naïvely, in retrospect, it was thought that Nature Reserves would be small and of little commercial interest or value. Neither would they be of interest to the general public and therefore they received relatively little publicity.

At the time of the establishment of these committees there was a strong feeling in Scotland that there should be separate Scottish committees. Parallel Scottish bodies were therefore also set up in 1947, both of which reported through another Command paper. It was the WLCSC report however, preceding the Scottish report that was by far the most influential as far as the future of nature conservation in Britain as a whole was concerned.

WLCSC's membership was composed, by and large, of the eminent scientists and biologists of the day, a number of whom would become household names through their authorship of books on natural history in the 1940s and 1950s that fed the growing public appetite for information on Britain's wildlife. For example, WLCSC's Chairman was the ecologist and behaviourist, Dr J S Huxley. Its Vice-Chairman was Professor A G Tansley (*Britain's Green Mantle* 1949), who took over the chair when Huxley moved to UNESCO as its Director, shortly after its first meeting. WLCSC's members included J A Steers (*The Sea Coast*, 1953), E B Ford (*Butterflies*, 1945; *Moths*, 1955), J S L Gilmour (*Wild Flowers* with M Walters, 1946) and E M Nicholson (*Birds and Men*, 1951) and its first Secretary was R S R Fitter (*London's Natural History*, 1945). Collins published all those titles in its popular and respected New Naturalist series, edited by chance by Huxley. Max (E M) Nicholson later became Director General of the Nature Conservancy and Tansley became its first Chairman. Coincidentally, a member of the first Nature Conservancy Committee was Professor W H Pearsall (*Mountains and Moorlands* 1950) and members of the first Scottish Committee included Dr Frank Fraser Darling (*The Highlands and Islands* with Dr J M Boyd, 1964) and C M Yonge (*The Sea Shore* 1949), whose books were also published in the same series. Boyd went on to become the Scottish Director of the Nature Conservancy in 1971. The founders of nature conservation in Britain were obviously keen to share their knowledge and enthusiasm for Britain's wildlife rather than to preserve it for an élite.

Command 7122 is critical to understanding the thinking behind the acquisition of Beinn Eighe, to the discussions of its management throughout this book and to the present view of the purposes of this and all other British National Nature Reserves. The paper's principal recommendation stated that a National Biological Service should be established to set up and manage Nature Reserves, to carry out research to advance our scientific knowledge and to make this knowledge 'available to be called upon by a variety of interests'. The proposed reserves 'must not only be maintained but used; and one of their most important uses will be as "field laboratories" for the study of wildlife and its control'.

One of the members of this Committee, E M Nicholson, held a pivotal position in the civil service at the time as a senior Civil Servant in the Ministry of Shipping. In 1945 he was headhunted for the position of Secretary to the office of Herbert Morrison (Lord President's office), the Deputy Prime Minister in Attlee's Government. This was the nearest department to a Ministry of Science that existed. Nicholson then, as well as being a member of the WLCSC and helping in the preparation of its report, was also the civil servant who advised Government what to do with it! Undoubtedly his influence played a large part in getting the 1949 Act establishing the Nature Conservancy through Parliament ahead of a queue of others of far more political importance. Nicholson, of course, was not merely an administrator; he was also an ornithologist who, in the 1930s, had studied at Oxford. There he had introduced the animal ecologist Charles Elton to the plant ecologist Tansley, so he was well aware of the developing science of ecology and the need for nature conservation in Great Britain.

The Scottish National Parks Committee, with a similar stratum of membership to that of its English counterpart, saw the prime purpose of National Parks to be to 'preserve the continuity of rural life in the communities concerned'. However, they considered that 'Much of the land of this (NP) quality … is in little need of preservation save perhaps from continual neglect'. Perhaps for this reason, but possibly more to do with the pressures that the Scottish landed establishment were able to bring to bear at the time, National Parks were not taken forward in Scotland. The Scottish Wild Life Conservation Committee (SWLCC), on the other hand, was in marked contrast to its English counterpart (WLCSC), with few individuals in the fields of ecology and nature conservation of the calibre of the latter committee. Their report was therefore very similar to, but much shorter than the English committee's report. Surprisingly, since most of its members were scientists, the same political pressures must have been successfully exerted on the SWLCC. Its report suggested that Scottish landowners had historically protected nature (through sporting management) and that it was the break-up of the large estates and the recent easier access to the Highlands by the public in private cars that were the main threats to nature.

Like the English Committee, SWLCC saw the establishment of a Biological Wild Life Service in Scotland as essential, not only for wildlife conservation, but '… for the economic development of natural resources', that included game, wildfowl and freshwater fisheries. The committee also foresaw that 'Success of nature conservation depends largely upon co-operation and the pursuit of a "good neighbour" policy'. However, the Committee did identify that 'Scotland's natural woodlands have suffered heavily on account of the acute timber and fuel shortage … [and] … there is a real and pressing need for the conservation of representative examples of the native woodland communities of Scotland, e.g. pine …'.

In their final joint report in 1949, which identified a number of potential Nature Reserves, the Scottish Committees recommended Coille na Glas Leitir as both a Nature Reserve and a National Parks Reserve within a National Park centred on

Loch Maree; Beinn Eighe in totality was not actually recommended. It described Coille na Glas Leitir as follows: '… a remnant of the native Caledonian Pine Forest. The wood has a steep northeastern aspect and rises into precipitous rocks at the 1000 foot (305 metres) contour. The numerous pines among the rocks may be regarded as an inviolable reservoir, from which regeneration may be expected. On the lower slopes havoc has been caused by wartime felling. However, much native pine remains … The area also includes an untouched example of raised bog.' The National Park was not taken forward and the final report recommended only that the boundary of the reserve should be fairly close to the periphery of the woodland.

For Coille na Glas Leitir and Beinn Eighe generally, a critical element of Command 7122 was the recognition that nearly all of the British countryside was modified by management and thus only 'semi-natural': management therefore needed to continue. It followed then that the management of reserves would need to be active, rather than *laissez faire*, and since so little was known about natural controls that sustain the delicate balance of nature, there would also need to be 'research and experiment'.

Following the publication of these Government reports, the Nature Conservancy was established by Royal Charter in 1949 with the following aims: 'to provide scientific advice on the conservation and control of the natural flora and fauna of Great Britain; to establish, maintain and manage nature reserves; and to organise and develop the research and scientific services'.

To understand the priorities of the Nature Conservancy staff of the first National Nature Reserve at Beinn Eighe, one must remember that the stated purposes of an NNR at this time emphasised scientific research and not public access or education, and to note also the earlier comments in the Scottish report on the perceived importance of traditional sporting management of estates.

The Scottish Conservancy

During the Second World War the Secretary of State for Scotland was the independently minded MP Tom Johnstone and it may well have been the political atmosphere he created that had led to the separate Scottish Committees. Their creation then, almost inevitably, led them to want an independent Scottish Nature Conservancy. Although, not surprisingly, this was not agreed to at Westminster, a measure of devolution was granted in the establishment of a separate Scottish Committee of the Nature Conservancy based in Edinburgh with its own Chairman and supported by its own Director and staff. To appease the Scots this Committee was ranked above all other Nature Conservancy Committees and responsible only to the Great Britain Committee, and it was agreed that purely Scottish matters would be dealt with only by the Scottish Committee.

Dr John Berry, a landowner and member of the Scottish Civil Service, was perhaps not the most obvious choice for the post of the first Scottish Director. The

Three Nature Conservancy
Directors in 1983:
John Berry, Joe Eggeling
and Morton Boyd.
Photo: SNH

best-known and most experienced ecologist in Scotland at the time was Dr Frank Fraser Darling. The author of several very popular natural history books, he was then working on his classic social and biological investigation into the problems of the West Highlands, which was to be published in 1954 as *West Highland Survey*. Darling, however, was *persona non grata* with the Scottish establishment, being particularly critical of, and outspoken about, the poor quality of land management by Scottish estate owners. He was not someone the Scottish Office thought it could control! Academics of the time also regarded the sort of applied and publicly accessible research that Darling carried out as somewhat inferior to academic research. Berry, on the other hand, was a member of the Scottish Landowners Federation and had already proved himself a steady and reliable hand as the environmental adviser to the Scottish Hydro Board. There he had got to know the Secretary of State and when the Nature Conservancy was being set up, Johnstone apparently persuaded his successor to appoint Berry, rather than Darling, as its Director, just before the appointment of the GB Director General. Johnstone was passionately opposed to the Scottish landowner aristocracy so his political judgement must have over-ruled his heart.

So when the Nature Conservancy (hereafter the Conservancy) was established in 1949 with Captain Cyril Diver, an amateur naturalist and civil servant, as the GB Director General, Berry was already in place. Apparently Diver made no bones about his opinion of Berry, telling him that if he had had *his* way Berry would never have been appointed Scottish Director. Nevertheless, Berry went on to serve very successfully as Scottish Director until the late 1960s, while Diver resigned his post after only three years.

Although Coille na Glas Leitir had been identified as a desirable Nature Reserve in the final report of the Scottish National Parks Committee, it was only one of many possible NNRs and there was no hint of its availability in 1949. In fact, at the third meeting of the Conservancy's Scottish Committee in October 1949, it was Morton Lochs in Fife, Flanders Moss in Stirling and Glen Doll in Angus that were all under consideration in Scotland: Beinn Eighe was not even on the horizon. The first and the last of these sites were in the course of being purchased by the Forestry Commission. Their representative on the Conservancy's Scottish Committee was their Scottish Director, Sir Henry Beresford-Pierse, who offered to sell on to the Conservancy those properties that it wished to declare as Nature Reserves.

While those possibilities were still under discussion, a year later on 10 November 1950, B R Feaver, of the Forestry Commission in Scotland, wrote to Berry concerning a woodland in the Beinn Eighe area. Noting that Coille na Glas Leitir was a proposed National Park Reserve on the list of possible Reserves that had been circulated around all government departments, he informed Berry that the Commission had been offered the opportunity to purchase a large area including the woodland. He enquired if the Conservancy would like to make a joint purchase with the Commission. Feaver included a map indicating the areas that the Commission thought might be planted and those that could not be planted. He suggested that perhaps the Conservancy could let him know what plans it might have for the management of the woodland and the surrounding area. From that moment Coille na Glas Leitir officially became Scotland's National Park Reserve One. Meanwhile in England, the Conservancy was pursuing another batch of potential reserves, one of the most important of which was Yarner Wood on Dartmoor, coincidentally another ancient woodland.

A few days later Feaver and Berry spoke on the telephone. Feaver suggested that the Commission might purchase the site and then re-sell to the Conservancy those areas the latter desired as a Reserve, just as had been proposed at other sites. However, Berry pointed out that all the plantable ground was in the area of the recommended National Parks Reserve, and that the Conservancy would be writing to the Commission to ask it to inform the owner of the Conservancy's interest in the area as a Nature Reserve. It is very clear from this correspondence between the two Government organisations and from that over the following year, that the Forestry Commission, the official forestry organisation in the UK, regarded the fledgling Conservancy very much as a young upstart. At every opportunity the Commission pressed its case for the initial purchase of the woodland and, failing that, offered to manage the site for the Conservancy. Perhaps it recognised this case for the precedent it would set, realising that unless it kept ownership and control of woodland management here, it would lose it in every other woodland NNR that would follow. Meanwhile, the Conservancy was made aware that it had to establish its own credentials quickly if it was not to be overshadowed.

The Scottish Director then wrote to Diver in London to inform him of the position. It could not have been other than a very excited man who wrote this letter to his boss and holder of the Conservancy's purse-strings. Berry was on the verge of establishing the very first NNR in the British Isles and he did not refrain from making use of a potential threat to the site to add a little urgency to the proceedings. Berry reported that a timber merchant was presently in the Loch Torridon area felling Caledonian pines and no doubt Diver would remember that many pines were felled around Coille na Glas Leitir during the War and that only a few still remained. Unfortunately, Berry also estimated the value of the timber on the site to be between £3000 and £10,000: the upper end of this estimate was possibly beyond the Conservancy's resources.

In his letter to Diver, Berry went on to say that Feaver, at the Forestry Commission, had pointed out that there were many deer in the area and, very prophetically, that he did not think the woodland would regenerate naturally, even if deer were excluded by fencing. He went on to say that the Forestry Commission would have to drain the ground and plant, probably using seed of local origin. Then there were further problems: the ground was very rough and rocky and it would no doubt be expensive to fence. Furthermore, the area of woodland was not just valuable for its timber, but for the shelter it gave to deer in hard weather. The area was part of a large deer forest and the owner would likely require unrestricted access for the deer.

In December 1950, R A Haldane (the Conservancy's Scottish Administrative Officer) wrote to Feaver and, couched in Civil Service language, included a statement of the Conservancy's powers of acquisition. It took the form of a reminder that 'when a proposed national reserve is concerned the Nature Conservancy's earlier claim qua government interest over other government organisations is already recognised …'. Haldane went on to say that there would be many more such sites, but reassured the Commission that through the National Parks Act (1949) there was a mechanism, already working in England, for the exchange of information on such sites between the Conservancy and Commission. In effect, he was pointing out to the Commission that the Conservancy's interest had precedence on the site anyway, whatever interest the Commission might have. The following day there was a meeting between the Scottish Conservancy and Forestry Commission staff, the former led by Berry and the latter by its Director, Beresford-Pierse – who was on the Conservancy's Scottish Committee, of course, and whose wife just happened to be a first cousin to Mrs Greig, the then owner of the woodland. The Scottish establishment is a small pond!

Berry's first concern was the possibility of the woodland being felled if the owner sold the timber. Beresford-Pierse reassured him that the Forestry Commission could hold up the felling licence. Then he tried to lean on the Conservancy, and Haldane records his words in the minutes of the meeting: 'Forestry Commission would be happy to meet Conservancy's needs if they want only indigenous species to be used. Possibly larch could be planted. If Conservancy acquired would they ask Forestry Commission to manage it?' Berry replied, naively in retrospect, that the Conservancy would probably say yes. His

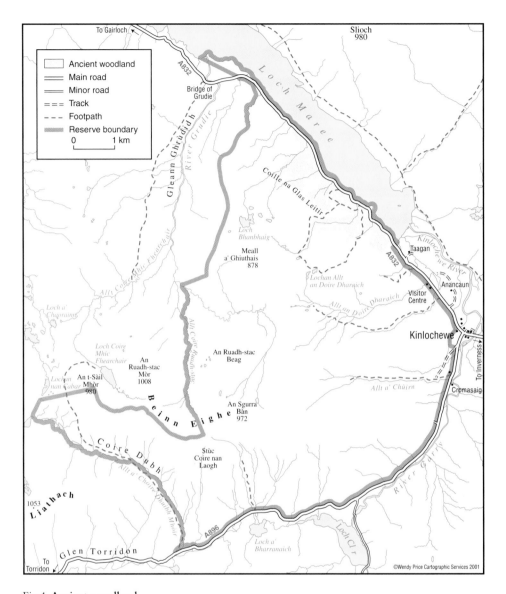

Fig 4 **Ancient woodland.**

principal worry following this meeting however, was with regard to the possible selling price, as the Conservancy, a government organisation, could offer only the District Valuer's valuation and this would likely be less than the owner could get from selling the timber. Would the Conservancy have to use its powers of compulsory purchase? Berry put all these points in a letter to the Conservancy's Director General that same day and included the fact that he understood that Mrs Greig not only wished to sell the wood, approximately 60 hectares (ha) plus a further 100 ha of plantable grounds, but apparently a further 4320 ha that

Deep heather
among the Scots pine
in Coille na Glas Leitir.
Photo: SNH

included the mountain of Beinn Eighe. However, there was no reason, nor intention, for the Conservancy to be interested in purchasing part of the mountain of Beinn Eighe. Little was known of its natural history, it was not on the list of proposed Reserves, it was a very large extent of ground and it was likely to be far more expensive than the Conservancy could afford.

A couple of weeks later in December 1950, at a meeting of the (GB) Conservancy which Berry attended, the Director General went some way towards placating the Forestry Commission: '(the) purchase in this case should be by the Nature Conservancy, but that any plantable portion not required for reserve purposes may be resold to the Forestry Commission'. But he made no suggestion that any additional land should be purchased. Otherwise, Berry was given the authority to proceed.

Stag on poor open and treeless ground.
Photo: R. Balharry

Meeting at Grudie

Berry then contacted Mrs Greig, the owner of Grudie (Grùididh, *gravelly burn*) Estate, to make arrangements to meet at her house by Loch Maree. It was a bad winter for snow in Scotland that year and he set off in his car for the north-west Highlands with chains at the ready in mid February 1951. However, as he later

Coille na Glas Leitir
in 1930
by Robert Adam,
prior to the last felling
and showing no signs
of regeneration.

wrote to Mrs Greig, he only got as far as north Perthshire and had to turn back lest he got stuck in a snowdrift!

Haldane must have been a model administrator for not only had he been unafraid to put a much larger government oganisation, namely the Forestry Commission, in its place, but he was also prepared to reprimand his own Director. He informed Berry that by taking his private car he had put them both in a potentially embarassing position *vis-à-vis* their boss. For the Scottish Director should have taken an office car and, to boot, if there had been public transport available, he informed Berry, he should have taken that! Haldane hoped that the Director General would not take them up on this breach of civil service regulations. Diver, no doubt, had more important things on his mind.

Two months after first hearing about the possible sale of Coille na Glas Leitir, Berry tried again and this time managed to get to Loch Maree and call on Mrs Greig. The meeting was very cordial and it became apparent that Mrs Greig was not only *not* interested in a Management Agreement or Lease, but that she *was* as

The old main road
along Loch Maree
around 1950
with Aultroy in the distance;
the scene today is woodland
on both sides of the road.

keen to dispose of the 4320 ha surrounding Coille na Glas Leitir as the wood itself. Part of the reason for wishing to dispose of such a large area around the wood was the fact that the only other real use of the surrounding ground was as a deer forest, which, without the woodland as winter shelter, was valueless.

As far as other uses of the proposed Reserve were concerned, Mrs Greig ran some sheep on the southern part of the ground in Glen Torridon, which she was keen to retain. In the event this ground became part of the Reserve and sheep grazing there officially ceased. For several years after, however, Mrs Greig continued to run sheep on Grudie, adjacent to the Reserve, which constantly crossed the unfenced boundary and caused problems for natural regeneration of Coille na Glas Leitir. Other grazing rights on the hill included those adjacent to the farm of Taagan (not itself on the property) whose tenant had a grazing right over 80–120 ha of unfenced hillside on the property, although that grazing right was seldom exercised. There were also other buildings on the property, one let to a Forestry Commission worker and another derelict.

To Berry's astonishment and delight, Mrs Greig put a value of only £4000 on the *whole* 4320 ha, including the woodland and its marketable timber. He could hardly believe his luck! According to Berry, such was the opportunity that was put in front of him, that he made a verbal offer of £4000 to Mrs Greig on the spot on 12 February and she accepted. He then telephoned Diver in London and told him that he had not only just bought the wood, but the mountain as well and all for the same estimated price. Apparently, Diver was furious and told him that he had had no right to do such a thing. Not only had he committed such a large sum of money without Diver's approval, but he had also purchased over 4320 ha around Coille na Glas Leitir when the Scottish Wild Life Conservation Committee had identified the need for only 290 ha. The Director General's embarrassment over Berry's action may also have been that, apart from Tansley, apparently no-one on the GB Committee had even heard of Beinn Eighe or had the remotest idea where it was, their attention being focused at that time on six possible reserves in England. Berry's response to this outburst from Diver, over what he considered a great bargain, was to say that if the Conservancy did not want it all, he would just purchase the additional hectares himself and then the Conservancy could buy the parts it required around the woodland *from him* when the official decision was finally made. Berry's recollection is that he had also hinted to his Director General that the price might have changed by then! Incidentally, as Peter Marren records in *England's National Nature Reserves* (1994), while Yarner Wood, one of England's first National Nature Reserves, cost approximately £77 per ha a year later, Beinn Eighe cost 74p per ha.

In March 1951 Berry reported to the Scottish Committee that the extra 4320 ha at Beinn Eighe were available and he was given the go-ahead to proceed. At the same meeting the Committee was informed that Morton Lochs, in Fife, was in the act of transfer from the Forestry Commission to Conservancy – either could have become Britain's first National Nature Reserve at this point. Following discussions with the District Valuer and a visit to the site by the Conservancy's GB Land Agent, Major B C Smart, in early April 1951, it was not until nearly mid-May that Mrs Greig formally accepted the offer of £4000 from the Conservancy with entry agreed for the 28th of that month. On his visit, Smart noted that 'One of the main deterrents to regeneration is the luxuriant heather growth and the thick carpet of moss and litter which tends to keep the seed away from any anchorage.' Smart, like Berry, had put his finger on one of the problems that was going to tax Conservancy ecologists for some years to come.

The final pieces of the jigsaw fell into place just before the purchase of Beinn Eighe was completed in September. Firstly, Beinn Eighe was scheduled by the Conservancy as a Site of Special Scientific Interest (SSSI), as are all National Nature Reserves. Secondly, Berry received a telegram from Pearsall on the GB Committee, suggesting that the two cottages, which had apparently been left out of the sale at Berry's request, should be included. There then followed a brief flurry of communications between Haldane, the Scottish Office solicitor and the agents acting for the Estate. Mrs Greig had no problems with their sale. One of these buildings, Aultroy Cottage would later become the Beinn Eighe NNR Visitor Centre, at present being upgraded in a radical reform of visitor facilities.

In later years, 1962 and 1973 respectively, an additional 23 ha of Scots pine along the lochside and 577 ha of adjacent National Trust for Scotland property in Torridon, were added by Management Agreement to the Reserve, bringing the total area of the reserve in 2001 to 4920 ha. The latter agreement made a more sensible boundary as far as deer movement was concerned and increased the opportunities for native pinewood restoration. Anancaun Farm and its buildings, as well as the farm at Taagan, were purchased by the Conservancy in 1953, but did not become part of the Reserve.

Declaration

On 22 November 1951, by public notice, Beinn Eighe was declared a National Nature Reserve, just one week after the purchase of Morton Lochs. Three days later reports on the event appeared in *The Times* and several of Scotland's national and local papers. *The Times* devoted several columns to the event, noting that the Coille na Glas Leitir woodland was 'scientifically the most notable thing in the reserve'. It also noted that one of the main objects of the Reserve was the opportunity for the study of 'natural conditions' over a wide range of altitude. Strangely there was no mention of red deer.

The Scotsman gave a shorter description of the natural history of Beinn Eighe but more space to the role of the Conservancy, mentioning its power to pass by-laws to safeguard the Reserve and its determination to prevent deer poaching or harm to wildlife. Prophetically, it hoped that the Reserve would 'add to the attractions of Wester Ross for the student of nature and the ordinary holidaymaker alike'. The *Glasgow Herald* gave space to two articles. The first

PUBLIC NOTICES

4 lines 30s. (minimum)

NATIONAL PARKS and ACCESS to the COUNTRY-
SIDE ACT, 1949.
DECLARATION of NATURE RESERVE.
BEINN EIGHE, PARISH of GAIRLOCH, COUNTY of
ROSS and CROMARTY.

Notice is hereby given in pursuance of Section 19 of the
above-mentioned Act that by the Beinn Eighe Nature
Reserve No. 1 Declaration, 1951, made on the 22nd day
of November, 1951, the Nature Conservancy declared
that the land extending to 10,450 acres or thereby comprising the eastmost portion of the lands and deer forest
of Beinn Eighe and Grudie in the Parish of Gairloch and
County of Ross and Cromarty and being the land shown
delineated by black lines and tinted pink on the map
attached to the said Declaration, has been acquired and
is held by the Nature Conservancy and is being managed
as a nature reserve.

Certified copies of the said Declaration with maps
attached have been deposited for public inspection free
of charge at the office of the Ross and Cromarty County
Council in Dingwall, between the hours of 9 a.m. and
5 p.m. on weekdays, except Saturdays, and between the
hours of 9 a.m. and noon on Saturdays, up to and including 31st December, 1951, and at the office of the District
Council of Gairloch at Poolewe, between the hours of
9 a.m. and 1.30 p.m. on all weekdays from 8th December
to 31st December, 1951, inclusive. Certified copies may
also be inspected at the offices of the Nature Conservancy
at 12, Hope Terrace, Edinburgh, 9, and at 91, Victoria
Street, London, S.W.1, between the hours of 9.30 a.m.
and 5 p.m. on weekdays, except Saturdays, and between
the hours of 9.30 a.m. and noon on Saturdays.

Dated the Twenty-second day of November, 1951.
F. BATH, Secretary of the Nature Conservancy.

Declaration of Beinn Eighe
as a National Nature Reserve
in *The Times*, 22 November 1951.

covered a similar area to *The Scotsman* but gave greater emphasis to the
opportunities for the study of wildlife of the area, which it was hoped would lead
to greater understanding of 'how the plants and animals lived'. The second,
briefer report was much more forward thinking, acknowledging that the
Conservancy's first duty was to provide advice on the conservation and control of
Britain's natural flora and fauna. It saw the findings of this work at Beinn Eighe as
also contributing to the benefit of forestry and agriculture, the mainstays of the
economy of the Highlands. More than any other newspaper, it also welcomed the
new opportunity for a relative freedom of public access to the mountains of
Scotland, an issue that was to grow in importance over the years.

The *Daily Express* concentrated on the outlawing of shooting and trapping,
reporting that the Nature Conservancy had asked neighbouring landowners to
tell their keepers to 'Shoo, but don't shoot', at animals that strayed outwith the
Reserve! The reporter asked some of the local people at Kinlochewe their opinion
and one shopkeeper hoped 'it will be a big success and bring many tourists'. The
Aberdeen Press and Journal thought it fitting that Britain's first National Nature
Reserve should be in the Highlands where much of the land was still untouched by
the hand of man, but on the other hand it noted that the disappearance of birds
and animals in the Highlands had been as marked as human depopulation over
the past hundred years.

Although the local newspaper, the *Highland News*, simply recorded the event
without any comment, the *Inverness Courier* devoted half its space to the
inhabitants of the village of Kinlochewe, the lack of employment, lack of mains
electricity and the perennial problems of marauding deer, hinting very broadly
that it, and the villagers, hoped the Conservancy would help solve them.

SCOTTISH NATURE RESERVE

RARE AND SPECTACULAR STRETCH OF HIGHLAND COUNTRY

By Our Special Correspondent

Below and opposite
Articles on Beinn Eighe
as a National Nature Reserve
in *The Times*,
22 November 1951.

To-day the Nature Conservancy, through its Scottish office, announces the purchase by private treaty of what is now the first large nationally owned nature reserve in Britain. It is to be called the Beinn Eighe Nature Reserve, from the mountain which dominates it, and it is situated at Kinlochewe, in Ross-shire.

The reserve consists of an approximate triangle of rough mountainous country in the angle of two roads leading from Kinlochewe north-west towards Gairloch and south-west towards Torridon. The Gairloch road boundary, some five miles long, lies for much of its way by the southern shore of Loch Maree, though there are some small pieces of land on the loch side of the road which are not included in the reserve. Along the Torridon road the reserve runs for some five or six miles. The third side of the triangle is about seven

miles long, runs across country, is marked by no road and, except where it runs along a stream or a sharp ridge of hill, is more or less arbitrary. The whole area amounts to 10,450 acres and forms a well-marked section of the great deer forest of Kinlochewe.

A particularly valuable feature of the reserve, in view of the fact that one of its main objects is the study of various natural conditions, is the considerable range of height included within it. At the shore of Loch Maree the height above sea level is only 32ft., and at the highest point inside the reserve it is 3,220ft. Beinn Eighe itself (pronounced Ben Ay, rhyming with "day," and meaning the Hill of the File, from the sharply toothed edges of some of its higher parts) occupies the south and south-west of the area. It is a hill of three main peaks, of which the highest, Ruadh-stac Mor (which, if a little very fragmentary Gaelic is to be trusted, is the Great Red Peak), 3,309ft., lies just outside the reserve. The other two, Ruadh-stac Beag (the Little Red Peak), 2,850ft., and Sgurr Ban (the White Peak), 3,220ft., are within its boundaries.

To the north of Beinn Eighe lies a second hill, Meall a' Chiubhais (the Hill of the Pines, pronounced Meowl e ewe-ish), 2,882ft. high, which forms the northern bluff of the reserve. Below its cliffs, stretching down to Loch Maree, lies Coille na Glas-leitire (the wood of the grey slope), the fragment of primeval Caledonian pine forest which is scientifically the most notable thing in the reserve.

Some of the place-names just quoted are clearly related to the geology of the place, which is of very great interest. The two chief rocks are the very early Torridonian sandstone and the Cambrian quartzite, and though the former is the more ancient formation it is, in certain places, found lodged, by some convulsion of the earth's surface, actually on top of the other. It is these two rocks which supply the colour element in the hill names—the Ruadh of the two red peaks of Torridonian sandstone, and the Ban of the "White Peak" with its screes of whitish quartzite, bare, to all distant appearance, of vegetation.

PINE FOREST

It is primarily the presence of the piece of ancient Caledonian pine forest that has led the authorities to establish the Beinn Eighe reserve, though the forest occupies only a small part of what has been acquired. Originally vast areas of Scotland were covered by forest, the almost total destruction of which has been the work of centuries. The Vikings began the devastation in the ninth and tenth centuries, burning the forest in order to destroy the natives who were hiding in it.

Great stretches of forest, again, were destroyed from the fifteenth to the eighteenth centuries, partly because the woodlands harboured wolves and robbers, partly in clan wars, partly to clear the ground for sheep, but chiefly perhaps for commercial purposes, especially to supply fuel for the smelting of iron—a piece of reckless improvidence, to which many thousands of bare Highland acres now bear witness. The fellings of two wars have, in our own time, still further reduced the remnant. Coille na Glas-leitire is not the largest surviving fragment of Caledonian pine forest, but it is of peculiar importance since the pines, as Sir Arthur Tansley, now chairman of the Nature Conservancy, noted some years ago, are seeding much more freely than they are in most other places. Certainly as one walks through the forest here there are pines of all ages, from seedlings upwards, to be seen in many parts of it.

The beauty and interest of these ancient scraps of woodland rest principally in the character of the pines, which are of the native Scottish form—*Pinus sylvestris* variety *scottica*—and differ in many small respects from the alien form of the species commonly planted by foresters. Among these characters are the smaller cones, redder branches, which have a greater tendency to grow in whorls, and shorter needles. Many of the old trees show a broad, flat-topped outline reminiscent of cedar trees—but there is very great variety of shape among them. Other woodland trees here are birch (which in patches is the dominant species), rowan, holly, an occasional oak, and, by the loch side, alder.

MOORLAND PLANTS

Most of the reserve, however, is rough treeless ground, variously boggy, the lower parts clothed in moorland vegetation which includes bell and cross-leaved heather, ling, bilberry, and *Vaccinium Vitis-idaea*, *Arctostaphylos Uva-ursi* (the rarer *A. alpina* grows on the high ground), bog myrtle, and some bracken. Above there are steep areas of scree, one or two little lochans at middle heights, and cliffs broken by ledges and by vertical fissures down which trickle small streams. These, combined with a wide range of altitude and humidity and with differences of soil, create a diversity of botanical habitats which are likely to repay the careful examination they will certainly get now that the area is to be devoted to the preservation and systematic study of its wild life.

Not that the vegetation of Beinn Eighe is unknown. That indomitable plant hunter, George Claridge Druce, paid it several visits, the first being in 1881. In spite of "truculent gamekeepers" he found a charming mountain willow herb, *Epilobium alsinefolium*, on Beinn Eighe in 1881; and as a result of other visits recorded for this hill *Arabis petraea*, *Polystichum Lonchitis*, *Salix herbacea*, *Carex rigida* and other good alpine plants, which, presumably, still grow there.

Doubtless it was the same stream, whose gully (as he wrote) sheltered Druce from the unfriendly eyes of the keepers in 1887, beside which your elderly and breathless Special Correspondent climbed, one misty November day, for some 900 feet, noting the huge sea-trout spawning in the lower pools, and the winter rosettes of the pretty white-flowered *Saxifraga stellaris* on the sandy shingles, and coming at last to a ridge where, at the head of a deep half-pine-clad hollow, a great corrie opened leading up to the screes and high jagged-toothed ridge of Sgurr Ban. By that peak wheeled the black dots that were two ravens—almost the only living animals, save the sea trout, seen on that particular walk. Birds seen on other days of a too short visit this month have been buzzards and peregrines, besides such comparatively small fry as hooded crows, dippers (by Loch Maree), stonechats, and among the pines long-tailed tits and gold-crests. The hill also has ptarmigan and red grouse. On the whole, however, the animal life does not flaunt itself before the casual eye. It is, nevertheless, there, and is of great interest. Both red and roe deer live on the reserve.

EAGLE AND WILD CAT

More important is it that Beinn Eighe is in the heart of country which is still the home of the most splendid of British birds, the golden eagle, and the fiercest and most powerful of British predatory mammals, the wild cat—though possibly these rather include the reserve in their range than inhabit it permanently. A more constant inhabitant is the lithe and agile pine marten, possibly the most graceful British mammal and now very rare, which lives in the forest area. The presence of this lovely animal is one of the things which make the formation of this nature reserve especially welcome, for the pine marten is a creature much persecuted, not only for the usual game-preserving reasons, but also for the value of its fur. Local rumour affirms that some dozen pine martens have been trapped round Beinn Eighe this year, and their furs sold at £10 apiece. Obviously one of the Nature Conservancy's problems is going to be the adequate protection of this animal.

The Nature Conservancy is believed to have done a great deal behind the scenes since it came into existence in 1949. Captain Cyril Diver and the nucleus of a staff which he has brought together, whether in London or in the Edinburgh Office directed by Dr. John Berry, are known to have done much preliminary and exploratory work towards the establishment of that chain of national nature reserves which is one of the Conservancy's main functions to establish and manage, as much for the advancement of scientific knowledge as for the preservation of what remains of the British heritage of wild life. Other nature reserves are believed to be under negotiation at present, but that at Beinn Eighe is the only one yet announced.

Scotland thus has the honour of taking, on this typical and spectacular stretch of wild Highland country, the first step in an experiment which may prove of the greatest value and interest. If it is an honour for Scotland, it is also a responsibility. The Beinn Eighe Nature Reserve is not a thing cut off absolutely from the country around it. There will certainly be matters which will have to be adjusted with neighbouring interests, and which will call for tact and understanding—on both sides—in the handling.

There will also be policies to be shaped in connexion with such things as public access—though the remoteness of this reserve should ease that particular difficulty as regards Beinn Eighe. For the moment naturalists of every grade will think it enough to rejoice that a beginning has been made—and on so generous a scale—with a project which may have seemed to some of its old advocates (and this pen, which was not the first, was pleading in coming cause 30 years ago) a weary time in coming into being.

A Nature Reserve

The country between Loch Torridon and Loch Maree in the north-west Highlands of Scotland is as wild and beautiful as any in these islands. Its great mountains of dark-red sandstone are among the very few on the mainland which cannot be climbed without using hands as well as feet and sometimes—if the climber is wise —a rope as well. From their stony peaks a man can look westwards to the Outer Isles and eastwards to the Cairngorms. In their rough corries deer graze in summer and the shadow of the eagle may be seen as it searches the ground for grouse and ptarmigan. It is a happy choice that part at least of this area should now have been purchased by the Nature Conservancy to become the first nature reserve in Britain.

The Beinn Eighe Nature Reserve, described in an article on this page, will not compare either in size or in the variety of its wild life with the great National Parks of Africa and North America. Yet it may help to save from extinction, and perhaps to increase, some of the rarest and most interesting of British birds and beasts. For this purpose the high ground is less valuable than the fragment of the old Caledonian forest included in its boundaries. This natural forest of Scots pines once stretched from Glen Lyon to Strathspey and from Glen Coe to the Braes of Mar; to-day only a few patches remain, of which the largest is the Forest of Rothiemurcus, in the Cairngorms. It is not only beautiful in itself with its old trees, red of bark or white with age, but was the home of most of the wild animals of Scotland. As the forest was cut or burnt some, like the wolf, were exterminated; others, like the red deer, changed their habits and became hardened to the rigours of the open hills; while others, again, clung to the few remaining patches. Of these it is too late to save the goshawk and the polecat, but, fortunately, not too late to save the pine marten, the capercailye, the crossbill, and the crested tit.

The pine marten, probably the rarest animal in Britain, is known to live in the Beinn Eighe Reserve and should now be fairly safe. The wild cat, too, which prefers the forest though it has found refuge in the treeless hills, is also found in the district. If the old pines seed themselves and the forest spreads, other birds and animals may come back, though the area is too small to be a really satisfactory sanctuary. The fate of these and many other birds and beasts depends less on the founding of this and other nature reserves than on the gradual education of the British people—landowners as well as crofters, townsmen as well as countrymen—to value and protect the wild life of these islands. Few of these creatures do as much harm as is alleged; all of them add beauty and interest to the countryside. Even those who have never seen and never hope to see a golden eagle in its native hills must surely feel that Britain would be a poorer place if this sight was extinguished for ever.

A PINE-CLAD GULLY in the Ross-shire Nature Reserve, with two of the peaks of Beinn Eighe showing above the trees.

All the newspapers, without exception, welcomed the establishment of Britain's first Nature Reserve and the protection that was going to be given to the wildlife of the Highlands, but other than protection and scientific study they did not have a clear idea as to what the Conservancy staff were actually going to do on Beinn Eighe – but then neither did senior staff at the Conservancy. In December 1951 an article appeared in the illustrated magazine, *The Sphere*, by Darling, arguably the person with the greatest knowledge of the natural history of the Highlands and its link with the region's economy. After explaining to his readers who and what the Conservancy was, and the essential difference between a National Park as established in England and a Nature Reserve such as Beinn Eighe, he immediately moved on to explain how little of the British Isles was in any way 'natural'. In other parts of the world there still existed wild country where nature could be left to look after itself, but in Britain, after a long history of pastoral and agricultural management, everywhere was affected by mankind and needed to be managed. Darling went on to extol the wildlife and geology of Beinn Eighe and ended his article with two key statements about the management of the Reserve. The first was that National Nature Reserves should be able to demonstrate improvements to the land through ecological research and management. He was speaking here from his wide experience of the impoverishment of Highland soils following a long history of mismanagement. The second – that fifty years later the present government body for nature conservation in Scotland, Scottish Natural Heritage, is still trying to get across – 'It cannot be too widely understood that conservation and wise land use are not in opposition, but are complementary in aim and practice.'

Both the GB and Scottish Committee members must have been very pleased that their first National Nature Reserve in Britain was so large and spectacular, even romantic – being set in the grandeur of the Highlands of Scotland with all its literary associations. It ensured good publicity and interest throughout the land. It also made for good magazine copy and fascinating radio material for people who did not have their own transport. In addition to the article in *The Sphere* there was an article in *Illustrated* (August 1952), a radio programme 'The Pattern in Nature' (1954), an article in *John Bull* (June 1956) and Dr J M Boyd's later article in the *Scottish Field* (1961).

Locally, attitudes were much more pragmatic: Would there be jobs? Would the Conservancy control the deer? Would it help with obtaining mains electricity? Brothers Malcolm and Iain MacDonald of Kinlochewe, later to have many dealings with the Conservancy, remember hearing of the declaration and wondering just who the Conservancy were? It seemed to the local community for a time that this was just another traditional estate owner: deer continued to be culled, vermin to be shot and people not encouraged on the hill.

Stalker, keeper and warden rolled into one

The first mention of staff for the new Beinn Eighe Reserve appeared in a report by Pearsall following a visit in August 1951, before the purchase of the Reserve had been completed. He saw the need for a Keeper in the winter months and a Forester/Warden in the summer. Commenting on this report, Darling emphasised that he should not just be a 'watcher or low-ground keeper', but should be a 'good type of stalker'.

The principal problem facing the Conservancy as a landowner in the Highlands in the 1950s was poaching, mainly of red deer, but also grouse, ptarmigan and hare. Even the pine marten was trapped for its pelt, which could fetch up to £10: a lot of money in those days. Deer poaching was partly a rather nasty commercial pursuit, with poachers travelling from a distance, and partly a local problem as, in the absence of deer fences and lack of food and shelter on the high, open ground, deer descended in the winter to maraud crops and even gardens in the village. It was also very hard to make a living in the crofting counties just after the Second World War. There was also the possibility that over-enthusiastic neighbouring gamekeepers, in the absence of a Keeper on the Reserve, might take the law into their own hands and control vermin, including pine marten and golden eagle. In addition, there were suspicions that the Conservancy people might not control foxes or crows themselves, an accusation that the Conservancy took pains to refute. Someone was needed who could carry out stalking and gamekeeping, a man of experience who would be respected by poachers and keepers alike. However, he should also be able to converse with the public and he was needed soon. At this time there were no plans for ecological management and so the first 'field' staff appointed by the Conservancy was to be a Keeper: the concepts of Rangers and Wardens had yet to come.

In September 1951, the Scottish Committee recommended the appointment of a Keeper. However, nothing was done immediately and from then until the following spring the Conservancy received a string of concerned letters and communications from surrounding landowners and the local police wanting to know when there was to be a man on the ground – the concern not being nature conservation, but game management. In fact, there already had been two men on the ground. At the time of declaration, Andrew Currie was the recently appointed Conservancy officer for most of the north of Scotland and should have made an appearance at Kinlochewe. Unfortunately, he was recovering from appendicitis and was unavailable. Another member of staff was therefore sought to be sent up from Edinburgh to hold the fort until Currie recovered. No scientist was available, so the very first person on the ground to be in charge of over 4000 ha of ancient woodland and mountain on Britain's very first National Nature Reserve was Jimmy Gunn. Gunn was a Caithness man, who just happened to be the caretaker of the Scottish headquarters at Hope Terrace in Edinburgh. Currie was the second when he had partly recovered from his operation. He remembers staying at Kinlochewe Hotel for six weeks and walking up and down the road for a number of days until he felt fit enough to venture into Coille na Glas Leitir.

The post of Keeper at Beinn Eighe was advertised in the press in March 1952. There were over fifty enquiries and the selected candidates were interviewed in April. The chosen candidate was Jimmy Polson, an experienced stalker and gamekeeper from the Lovat Estates, who was informed of his success that day. Five days later Polson was officially appointed as the Conservancy's first field staff, just beating the gamekeeper of Yarner Wood in England, who became the Warden for that Reserve the following month. The search to find local accommodation for Polson began immediately. In June the Conservancy obtained a lease of the farmhouse adjacent to the Reserve at Anancaun for six months at a rent of £1 per week, but was unable to purchase the building until November. Until then, Polson, who took up his duties on the Reserve on 16 June, had to camp-out in the old, leaking farmhouse, repairs to which could not be carried out until the purchase was completed. It was to be several months before an increasingly impatient Polson and his wife were to be dry and comfortable.

Doire Darach,
one of the gorge remnants
of pinewood.
Photo: J. MacPherson / SNH

3 Ecologists and foresters 1952

'Except in grooves of streams, armpits of hills,
Here's a bald, bare land, weathered half away.
It pokes its bony blades clean through its skin
And chucks the light up from grey knucklebones,
Tattering the eye, that's teased with flowers and stones.'

Norman MacCaig, 'Treeless Landscape'

What to do?

Up to now all had been theory and principle. Now, at last, the committees and eager new staff of the Nature Conservancy were faced with their very first practical challenge. The moment had come when the Conservancy had to begin setting benchmarks in the field of nature conservation management that would distinguish it from all other Government 'countryside' bodies. And it was not only management on the ground that had to be faced. Suddenly, the Conservancy was confronted by neighbours, landowners, local authorities, the press and a whole range of interested parties with whom it was going to have to deal. Beinn Eighe National Nature Reserve was to become the test bed for many processes and structures, including the administration of the Conservancy itself.

The responsibility for this first step in Scotland lay with a fairly disparate group of people on the Scottish Committee, composed of naturalists, ecologists, academics and foresters, seasoned with a dash of the Scottish establishment and aristocracy. The discussions and arguments behind the decisions that were taken in the early years of Beinn Eighe, particularly in relation to the woodland, are of great interest, for in the end, they established the Conservancy's identity and its *modus operandi*. This chapter, therefore, is devoted entirely to the Reserve's first full year and the central dilemma of how to fulfil the primary aim of regeneration of the woodland, a task that had no precedents and that was to culminate several years later in the first Beinn Eighe Management Plan (1957).

Dr Heather Salzen (née Fairlie), a botanist, visited Beinn Eighe in early May 1951, following the successful negotiations of Dr Berry, but before the Reserve was purchased. After Berry and his secretary, Salzen was only the third member of staff to be employed in Scotland in January 1950, at which time all three worked in one rented office room in the centre of Edinburgh. Shortly thereafter, the building at Hope Terrace – still Scottish Natural Heritage's (SNH) centre of operations today – was purchased for twice the cost of Beinn Eighe. Salzen went on to play an important role alongside Donald McVean, an influential figure at Beinn Eighe, for the next three or four years and remembers especially the excitement of being in the vanguard of this pioneering band of ecologists and entering Coille na Glas

Pioneer surveyors
around 1950
above Allt a' Chùirn.
Photo: SNH

Leitir for the first time. Here, in a country otherwise dominated by open moorland of limited diversity – Darling's 'wet desert' – was an oasis of luxuriance and shelter, an intricate architecture of trees set among native woodland herbs and ferns. The tallest and grandest of which – thick-boled and red-barked – had large spreading limbs and had obviously only reached their grand and spreading structures over a long period of time. The atmosphere was one of tranquillity and age, and she immediately sensed that this was a very special and precious place. Salzen and others who have followed all recall the immense responsibility and privilege they felt in contributing to the pinewood's survival.

In her report of that visit, Salzen noted that there *was* natural regeneration at the edge of Coille na Glas Leitir, but that undoubtedly grazing pressure from deer, sheep and the occasional goat was suppressing seedling survival. G N Sale (forester for the Scottish Conservancy), who visited later that month, made similar comments, adding that unless regeneration was allowed there would be a continuing degeneration of the wood. Like Salzen, he thought that removal of grazing was all that was required. One further comment he made was picked up by Steven and Carlisle (1959) and later by others: '… the particular race of pine found in Coille na Glas Leitir is undoubtedly adapted to these [mild and wet] peculiar conditions.'

Two months later in July 1951, Professor Pearsall and Dr Verona Conway, the Chief Botanist from the London staff, made the first description of the plant communities of the Reserve. They found nothing exceptional only ample evidence of woodland degeneration: peat slumping where trees may have been removed, signs of muirburn in the wooded area and, on the lower slopes and south of Allt a' Chùirn (*burn of the cairn*) abundant evidence of pine in the peat. They emphasised in their conclusion that the first priority for work on the Reserve must be a full biological survey. There was obviously far more of nature conservation interest on the Reserve than just the woodland, however immediate attention was to be predominantly focused on it. They then foresaw a need to set up plots for monitoring future changes following management and a need for woodland regeneration experiments and studies of the various biological and physiographical features, including the climate.

Following their brief survey, the influential Pearsall produced a report entitled *Draft Recommendations for General Policy of Management*, incidentally calling the Reserve the Kinlochewe Nature Reserve. As his were the very first comments of someone who had devoted a lifetime to the study of mountains and moorlands, they are extremely important, particularly in regard to the management discussions held by several members of the Conservancy Committees and staff on their visit a year later and to the actual management that was carried out at Beinn Eighe from 1953 onwards. His report was very influential, neatly summarising the conditions and extent of the remaining native woodland.

Noting that the reserve was, 'fully representative of the natural biological units found in the N W Highlands, including striking mountains, vestigial woodlands of pine and birch and intervening moorlands.' Pearsall went on to say that, 'The particular interest of the Kinlochewe area, however, lies in its possible merit as a deer forest *and* in the existence of vestigial woodland of pine and birch'(our emphasis). 'The woodlands,' he said, 'are valuable for three reasons: as surviving relics of the old Caledonian pine forest, as part of the biological unit of the deer forest supplying necessary winter harbourage for deer, and scientifically of interest as part of a system including woodland and the traditional moorland types which replace it in a wet climate.' From the beginning Pearsall recognised the inseparable link between the deer and the woodland: that the one shapes the other.

How many fences, where and when?

Unfortunately, as Pearsall went on to say in his recommendations, the now reduced area of woodland was even more of a magnet for red deer in the winter and the increased grazing pressure meant that the few seedlings that germinated were not surviving to perpetuate the woodland. The woodland required protection from grazing while it regenerated, there needed to be a cessation of burning and there needed to be some judicious planting. The only way to protect young trees from grazing was to enclose them with a deer-proof fence. He then identified the three remaining areas of ancient woodland, namely the large block centred on Coille na Glas Leitir and the ravine woods in Allt a' Chùirn and Allt an Doire Dharaich, pointing out that: 'a good deal of the low ground is potential woodland and could sooner or later revert to this ...' However, Pearsall had also said at this point that, apart from the woodland at Allt a' Chùirn, further enclosures should wait until Coille na Glas Leitir had regenerated to provide sufficient shelter for the deer forest. This was a rather optimistic view, as we shall see.

The next question concerned how much land to fence. If the whole area were fenced, wintering deer would be forced onto other low ground woodland, arable land and into Kinlochewe itself. The alternative was to fence several small areas in phases, always leaving some woodland open for deer shelter and, Pearsall suggested: 'The need to do a certain amount of thinning of the herd of deer will no doubt arise.' However, he never suggested that another solution, avoiding fencing altogether, would have been to reduce deer numbers to the point where the grazing pressure was in balance with regeneration. To understand why not, we need to step back fifty years to a period before hill walking, access and the perilous state of our native forests had become common topics of public concern and when it was accepted that stalking and grouse shooting took precedence over all other activities on Highland hills. At that time only someone like Darling – who coincidentally supported the idea of a series of small enclosures – would challenge such an assumption and suggest that deer numbers at Coille na Glas Leitir be reduced to a ratio of 2.5:100 ha. That Pearsall saw the Kinlochewe Reserve as a deer forest *with* a vestigial wood was simply a reflection of the times. Fencing out deer from relatively tiny areas was an acceptance of the traditional view that red deer had priority over woodland on the hill.

Salzen made a second survey of Beinn Eighe in October 1951 and she noted that on Cnoc na Gaoithe (*knoll of the wind*), the rocky ground which was now sparsely covered in vegetation had once supported woodland and surmised that: 'Erosion must have been very rapid after removal of the trees to reduce the peat to its present thin state.' She also noted that: 'Small pines 6–10 inches are numerous, but all are severely grazed back and stunted. Many are prostrate and evidently quite old. Exposure may well be a factor here preventing normal growth as well as grazing by deer.' This was the 'inviolable reservoir' described in the report of the Scottish Wild Life Conservation Committee four years earlier. In fact, it was no reservoir at all but a scattering of stunted trees going nowhere.

**Kinlochewe
at the foot of Beinn Eighe.**
Photo: SNH

Open, potential pinewood
around remnant woodland
in Allt a' Chùirn;
footpath to the ridge
on the right.
Photo: SNH

In the same month, the Conservancy's Scottish Committee met and discussed Beinn Eighe. Beresford-Pierse of the Forestry Commission argued against small areas of fencing as a method of relieving grazing pressure and encouraging natural regeneration in Coille na Glas Leitir. Such an approach would be much too expensive and at 0.4 ha a year, as had been suggested, it would take between thirty and forty years to complete coverage of the whole woodland. Anyway, the Commission had been trying to regenerate woods naturally for twenty years without much success. He then went on to say that, 'The Forestry Commission too, have an interest in these woodlands because it is their duty to achieve the maximum productivity of the woodlands of the country of which this forms part.' He was also against the Conservancy having a tree nursery, as had been mooted, as this required forestry skills. He concluded with a proposal that the Forestry Commission should take over 120–160 ha of the main area of woodland to relieve the former of costs. This was a further take-over bid by the Commission for any 'woodland' operation before the Conservancy had even got off the ground and it was not to be the last. His proposal was not accepted by the meeting.

On a lighter note, in early 1952 Berry had a letter from the Forestry Commission requesting permission to collect Scots pine cones at Beinn Eighe. In giving permission he requested that the Commission give notice in advance, for, he reminded them, the last time they had made their collection – by blasting the high cones off the trees using a shotgun – the gunshots had been misinterpreted as the sound of poachers and set off an alert that roused the local police.

Strong opinions on management

At a meeting of the Scottish Committee in March 1952 Beresford-Pierse raised the matter of the future management of Coille na Glas Leitir, adding, perhaps a little threateningly, 'Lord Home [Scottish Minister] is particularly anxious that there should be an increase in afforestation in the North West. He wants the whole of the area from Beinn Eighe to Gairloch to be surveyed. Could we know therefore what is to happen about the woodland?' It was agreed then, and later confirmed at the next meeting of the Committee, that staff and members should visit the Reserve before making any commitment to management policy.

In July 1952, therefore, eight months after its declaration, an august group of members of the GB Nature Conservancy Committee, Scottish Committee and staff met for the first time on the new Nature Reserve. The discussions centred on Coille na Glas Leitir, the reason for its acquisition and its management. Of the group of ten, a third were botanical ecologists and another third foresters. Berry, the Scottish Director, was present and drew up the report, but unfortunately, as we shall see, Diver, the Director General, was absent. What occurred at this gathering illustrates the strong and sometimes divergent points of view of the great and the good when they came, with their own agendas, to address the practical issues of nature conservation management of Britain's first National Nature Reserve. Their deliberations raised the very fundamental question as to how the woodland management policy of the Conservancy would differ from that of the Forestry Commission, and forced them to address the very principles of ecological management.

Having already been over the ground the previous year and made several suggestions as to management, Pearsall led the early discussion within and around Coille na Glas Leitir, pointing out the degeneration of the soils both on the knolls and slopes where the woodland had been felled during the war. He emphasised that action was required urgently if the moribund wood was to be regenerated. All agreed that the various factors preventing regeneration included shallow and poor soils, thick mats of moss, heather and other herbage, over-grazing and possibly poor drainage. Pearsall, unfortunately, was unable to stay for the discussions, but before he left he pointed out that the regeneration of Coille na Glas Leitir was only part of the challenge: 'The second part of the problem is the re-creation of forest on other parts of the Reserve which once were forest, but which have now become almost, or completely, treeless.' The woodland remnants occupied only a small area of the low ground and there was obviously going to have to be a great deal of discussion as to how this might be achieved.

In those discussions it was accepted that the first priority was the protection and regeneration of Coille na Glas Leitir itself and it was agreed that most of the woodland should be fenced, although a small area where there were signs of regeneration should be left outwith the fence, as a control experiment. The Conservancy files of the time make it clear that Berry wrote a draft report of the discussions, which he then circulated, to the participants for comments. Unfortunately, this draft no longer exists, but it is apparent from some of the comments and from the final text of the report that there were two conflicting approaches to the problem of woodland 're-creation'. One was led by the foresters, supported by the Earl of Wemyss, who spoke in terms of timber, felling, drainage, unsuitable ground for planting, exotic species and control of birch. For example, Beresford-Pierse again suggested that the Forestry Commission could take over and do all the planting for the Conservancy and that the resultant timber would belong to the Commission.

The other faction appears to have been led by Pearsall, supported by Darling and Professor C M Yonge. Darling was against replanting in principle and in practice. Yonge, in a letter of comment to Berry, said that considerable further investigation and experiment were needed before the 'peculiar interests of the Conservancy, can be decided'. In the absence of Pearsall from the final discussions, the group agreed that there should be artificial planting, of indigenous species only, in groups throughout Coille na Glas Leitir, after fencing. It was also agreed that the Commission should establish experimental pilot plots on Conservancy ground in Glen Torridon where trees were all but absent. These would include exotic species planted as shelter for Scots pine, which would later be removed. The report recognised that Glen Torridon had very poor soils and was very exposed to the prevailing wind and that 'Only a violent upheaval of the subsoil could rectify such conditions and make the land able to grow healthy trees.' This last angle, promoted by the Commission, was strongly supported by the Earl of Wemyss. In a letter of comment to Berry on the draft report he stated that since only Coille na Glas Leitir was recognised as of natural interest and the rest of the Reserve was only bought because 'it was thrown in cheap', there was no reason why the latter 'must be "naturally" treated'. Conway had Berry add a rider to this part of the report pointing out that some of the bogs were of great botanical interest and should be left unplanted. The recommendations of the group, however, were for fairly rapid and intense interventionist management – a far cry from the original conceptions of Pearsall and Diver. A concerned Yonge added in his subsequent minute to Berry, 'I am by no means certain that what Pearsall suggested and what Sir Henry was prepared to do really amounted to the same thing. There is a gulf between the outlook of the botanical ecologist and that of the forester.'

A very positive outcome of this first visit of Committee members was the unanimous agreement to establish a small field station with accommodation for research workers and for training ecology students at Anancaun, once the Conservancy purchased the buildings. This quite radical proposal was to have an immense influence on Beinn Eighe's future, leading to the participation of hundreds of students and volunteers from all over Britain in the Reserve's management.

Berry then sent a copy of his revised report of this visit to Diver, just prior to a meeting of the Scottish Committee in September 1952, at which Pearsall – the architect of the proposals for planting by hand in as natural a manner as possible – again was not present. Diver, who was an amateur naturalist and not an interventionist in nature conservation management, was a little upset by the report, to put it mildly. He and Berry must have had a discussion about the conclusion of the report on the telephone, disagreeing strongly, and Berry must have complained that he was being bullied, for Diver's written response to the report opened with

Margaret Wallace, Maureen Polson, Peter Wormell, Ken Wallace and Donald McVean.
Photo: R. Balharry

'You *are* being bullied'. He attacked his Scottish Director and the report on two counts. The first concerned internal procedures – here was a group of individuals acting as if they were the management committee – this was a recipe for chaos. Berry hastened to reassure him that the report was simply a summary of the opinions of the group and not an approved policy for management. Secondly, Diver pointed out that virtually all of the management proposed by the Committee members could equally well be carried out by the Commission and he could not see how any of the proposals would further the aims of the Conservancy. Diver was concerned as to how their proposals might be viewed by the Scottish Office (who would also see the report as part of the Scottish Committee papers). He pointed out that fencing most of Coille na Glas Leitir would reflect adversely on the Conservancy as a deer manager because the displaced deer would create problems on neighbouring land. He was also particularly concerned with the proposals for the remainder of the Reserve below the tree line. Had that ground not been purchased to allow study of the natural conditions of the wide range of habitats it contained? Why was the Conservancy going to spend so much of its limited funds creating a forest? And where was the baseline survey and research that should be carried out before any action was considered? Among the several counter proposals he put to Berry, apart from the fact that all this needed to be discussed at the next Scottish Committee, was that Darling should be invited to assess the deer situation at Beinn Eighe at the earliest opportunity as part of his

Scottish-wide red deer survey that was just starting. Diver's vision for the Conservancy's activities in the woodland was set out quite explicitly in this short extract from his long and detailed minute to his Scottish Director: 'The Coille na Glas Leitir area presents first class opportunities for the long-term study of natural regeneration and the nature of natural tree growth in the conditions there obtaining ... The fundamental question that awaits detailed enquiry is: How does a natural wood perpetuate itself as an ecological entity?'

Berry's reply came straight from the heart: 'The hopes I had a couple of months ago that I was beginning to learn how ecologists view an area such as Coille na Glas Leitir, have been somewhat shaken by discovering how fundamentally opposed eminent ecologists appear to be on the subject ...' There were not only problems with the adamant opinions of the foresters, the ecologists were also split between those who thought immediate action was required to save the wood and those who thought it could be left for ten years without any further threat to its future.

The Scottish Committee decides

Diver's intervention created quite a stir in the Edinburgh office. Just when Berry thought he had the general agreement of the eminent scientists, ecologists and foresters, Diver threw it all back at him. The meeting of the Scottish Committee on 9 September 1952, which was largely given over to discussions on Beinn Eighe, was an extraordinary affair. In the records of these meetings, which always covered numerous agenda items, each item was normally reported in no more than a paragraph. The record of this particular meeting devoted a whole page to what must have been a heated debate, on how to begin restoring Coille na Glas Leitir.

Diver 'stressed the need for a preliminary survey of the topography, the vegetation, the degree of destruction, and the deer population in Coille na Glas Leitir before any decisions were taken to fence or plant.' Beresford-Pierse said it needed to be planted; Professor Ritchie 'would like to see recreation', Professor Walton said: 'artificial means must be taken to encourage regeneration if essential elements of the pine forest ground flora were not to be lost'. Lord Wemyss wanted to: 're-establish it without delay ... [it] ... would appeal to general public.' The feeling of the pro-fence lobby was that even if the woodland was fenced immediately it would take years for any change to occur to the ground vegetation. They felt it should be fenced straight away and the Conservancy should get on with the collection of Scots pine cones and the raising of seedlings.

Walton, seconded by Beresford-Pierse, moved that 'an area of not less than 200 acres be fenced'. Dr McArthur of the Macaulay Institute, seconded by Arthur Duncan, moved a counter proposal that 'nothing be done until a botanical and soil survey had been carried out'. Those for fencing included Beresford-Pierse, Professors Peacock, Ritchie, Walton and Yonge and Lord Wemyss; against were Duncan, McArthur and Professor Matthews. The motion was therefore passed as a majority decision that 44 ha should be fenced to exclude grazing and encourage natural regeneration.

It was then agreed that if natural regeneration did not occur in the enclosure there should be some baring of the soil and sowing of pine seed collected from the wood. Only if this was unsuccessful might there then be some random planting of native stock. Such management would require the establishment of a nursery and the raising of plants that would take two to three years. There was therefore a minimum period of several years available to see if natural regeneration would occur while surveys were completed. Apart from that there was no decision taken concerning the long-term future management policy.

A change of leadership

At this point Diver, who had perhaps found the post of Director General very different from what he had expected, was in the act of resigning. Apart from reining in the Scottish Committee over Beinn Eighe, his major contribution to the Nature Conservancy had been the foresight to see that the future Conservancy must be a professional and respected body. He therefore had ensured that the very best scientific minds were employed and trained to take over in the next few years, men such as Derek Ratcliffe and Duncan Poore. His resignation left the Government desperately looking for someone to take over. Diver's replacement had to be a very able leader and administrator with some grasp of ecology and nature conservation – someone who would pull the Conservancy together and shape it for the future. There were very few people worldwide who had the desired qualities and qualifications and all those selected apparently refused the offer. Finally, Sir Arthur Duncan, Chairman of the Conservancy, turned to Max Nicholson on the GB Committee and said that either the whole thing should be wound up or Nicholson should take over. The latter was then finding his job in the Lord President's office under the new Government carried much less responsibility than it had under Herbert Morrison. He therefore resigned from the post of Secretary and took over as Director General of the Nature Conservancy in late 1952. Almost immediately he requested a statement of the views of the Scottish Committee on the Beinn Eighe Management Policy and at the same time drew up a structure for Management Plans to be followed on all National Nature Reserves.

Early the following month, in October 1952, Salzen returned to Beinn Eighe with Donald McVean. McVean was a dedicated and tireless plant ecologist who had just been appointed to the Conservancy in Scotland and who was at the time responsible for the West of Scotland from Glasgow to Ross-shire. He was to play a key role in future research experiments in natural regeneration at Beinn Eighe. The two mapped the trees in Coille na Glas Leitir and noted that they could find no pine seedlings less than six years of age, in other words, no seedlings had survived since the wartime felling. Later that month McVean returned for a more intensive survey. He made several observations regarding the reasons for the lack of natural regeneration including poor light intensity in the shaded parts of the woodland and noted that 'Regeneration is almost certainly prevented by the luxuriant growth of … mosses which may even kill the heather.' He concluded: 'It will probably be extremely difficult to rehabilitate the Coille na Glas Leitir. Climatic conditions seem to be completely against the growth of pine at the present day, and the treatment that the wood has received has not helped the situation. Fencing certain areas can scarcely do any harm but immediate results should not be expected … Any programme will have to be regarded on a very long-term view since certain forestry short cuts to success are denied us.' These final remarks referred to commercial forestry techniques.

This report must have put a damper on any optimistic view within the Conservancy that regeneration of Coille na Glas Leitir would be relatively straightforward and that very soon Beinn Eighe National Nature Reserve would demonstrate the benefits of nature conservation management to politicians and the public alike. It should have prepared all involved for a long haul and was a warning shot across the bows of those who wished to see commercial Forestry Commission-type intensive intervention. It also, to an extent, challenged the views of people such as Pearsall who felt, because of the apparently deteriorating ground conditions, that urgent action was required to restore the woodland. That Pearsall's preferred management included further fencing and planting is made clear in a letter written nearly ten years later in 1961 to Dr Morton Boyd regarding proposals for a further large enclosure: 'I am all for greatly increasing the protected area at Beinn Eighe. My original suggestion was to fence the area including and east of the present enclosure and to the lake end and to replant and regenerate the wood as quickly as possible.'

It must have seemed to Berry, towards the close of 1952, following that lively Scottish Committee meeting, that at last there was something on which to base general agreement and that management was proceeding – except for a management policy. The only hiccups to surface involved minor internal territorial squabbles, problems typical of a partly devolved organisation in its early life. Irritations such as the Director General in London unilaterally encouraging academic research without consultation with Scotland and visiting 'experts' from England producing reports that told Scottish 'experts' nothing new were commonplace. However, at the Scottish Committee meeting in January 1953 some larger spanners were once again thrown into the works, this time by heavyweights from London. Sir William Taylor of the GB Committee questioned whether Coille na Glas Leitir really was an ancient piece of Caledonian pinewood: how did the Conservancy know that it had not been planted? If it was not an ancient wood the area should be drained and this would require a dam! Anyway, even if it were ancient, would it not be easier to conserve a pinewood somewhere else in Scotland? It is not difficult to imagine the consternation such queries must have caused some of the members of the GB and Scottish Committees, never mind the Scottish staff. Shortly thereafter in a memo to Berry, Salzen pointed out that there were no indications that the trees had been planted and, in a sardonic addition, that in any case this was probably the last place anyone would try. The meeting of the Committee ended therefore with the return to a number of fundamental questions: whether it would be practical to fence, drain and plant, what the cost of this would be, whether the effects on the vegetation of such intensive intervention would be acceptable, whether regeneration was a matter of urgency and what other survey work was required?

A couple of days later Nicholson met with Salzen and they produced a paper recognising that Coille na Glas Leitir was in a poor state and that the Conservancy aim must be to 'restore it to a viable and flourishing state', but establishing also that since 'there is some uncertainty and difference of opinion regarding the practicability of satisfactory regeneration', that a 'high priority should be given to survey and experimental work aiming at establishing a sound basis for a long term programme [of restoration].' This paper was put forward to the next Scottish Committee meeting in March 1953 with a number of recommendations for research including soil and deer surveys. The recommendations included the proposal for a 44 ha enclosure with Coille na Glas Leitir (see Fig 6 and App 1) between Alltain Ruadh (*red-brown burn*) and Allt Bhanbhaig (*little burn that is like a pig*) for protection and experiments on grazing effects. A second proposal was that there should be collection of pine seed from the wood and that Salzen and McVean should take this forward. The area for the enclosure chosen by McVean included a variety of vegetation types such as open pine wood, open moribund birch wood, treeless heathery banks and poorly drained flats of deer grass and purple moor grass. At long last, under the firm guidance of Nicholson, it appeared that a management policy was in place.

However, before we briefly scan the range of survey and research that was stimulated, both by the paper at the above meeting and by Diver in his response to

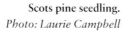

Scots pine seedling.
Photo: Laurie Campbell

the proposals of the Committee members who visited Beinn Eighe in July 1952, we should perhaps return to Beresford-Pierse's final throw of the Forestry Commission dice. He was obviously disturbed that the Conservancy was proposing to carry out woodland research, which he saw as the fief of the Commission. In a letter to Berry earlier in the year he implied that the proposed Conservancy research was the same as that of the Commission and that the former should really be filling in the gaps (of Forestry Commission research). Salzen and McVean responded vigorously to this suggestion (in a memo to Berry) pointing out, among other things, that the Conservancy's research was 'ecological' and not 'silvicultural'. In that response McVean repeated a point made earlier by Sale, the Conservancy's forester, that the trees of Coille na Glas Leitir appeared to be adapted to unfavourable climatic and soil conditions and were therefore probably of a local race of Scots pine. McVean went on to say, 'The wood should not be regarded as a fragment of typical primeval pine forest.' This is a key point that is still often misunderstood by not only native woodland managers and their critics, but of managers of any ancient habitat, such as mountain scrub or tall herb communities. McVean was pointing out that what had survived was only the battered remnants of hundreds of years of mismanagement. He then went on to reiterate what he had said before and would say again, that 'there [should not] be any attempt to force the wood to resemble some preconceived idea of pristine wood by planting and other expensive operations. Experiments should however be directed towards finding ways in which the ill effects of former mis-use can be mitigated and the full biological potential of the habitat realised.' Despite these insights, as we shall see, future Conservancy staff were to find themselves pressurised into just that 'preconceived idea' McVean had warned against.

Tansley's Bog
in the pinewood
of Coille na Glas Leitir.
Photo: J. MacPherson / SNH

4 Survey, experiment and gooseberries 1953–57

'As a result of four years observations on natural pine regeneration throughout the Highlands I have to agree with
the Forestry Commission's conclusions that "at best, unaided natural regeneration is erratic, undependable, and a
long drawn out process".'

Donald McVean, 'Highland Pine Forests:
Methods of Regeneration' (1957)

Early survey and research

But what of all the other survey work that had been proposed? It came in a rush
of enthusiasm in those early days. In 1952 Glasgow University contributed a
comprehensive collection of plants. Salzen then drew up a list of bryophytes and,
with McVean, a vascular plant list. The latter then produced a macro-lichen list in
1953. In the summer of 1952 P J Newbold, from University College London, more
closely examined the bog vegetation that Pearsall and Conway had briefly
surveyed the year before. Currie and Betty Garden (Aberdeen University)
compiled lists of breeding birds. A list of water beetles was added by Ann Gordon
(librarian at Hope Terrace), who then added to and analysed an earlier collection
of spiders by Salzen. It is an illustration of the paucity of previous systematic
surveys of the natural history of the area that of the thirty-two spiders collected
an astonishing twenty were new records for the county. O W Richards carried out
an invertebrate survey and woodland insects were covered in a brief survey by G
H Thompson of Oxford University in July 1953. The latter, commenting on the
poor weather and lack of insect activity, drily noted one of the hazards of working
in the North-West Highlands in summer, 'Only the midges were undeterred by
rain or cold; they disported themselves with abandon in all kinds of weather
except during the brief appearances of the sun.' Another scientist, carrying out a
small mammal survey visited that July too, and he also noted that there was not
a dry day during the whole of his visit. Beinn Eighe may be a romantic place, but
it had its share of hardships to be endured.

One of the most important scientific events was the establishment in 1953 of
the official climatological station at Anancaun, by the Conservancy's
meteorologist Frank Green, with its daily weather monitoring, which continues in
operation to this day. He also set up rainfall gauges in Coille na Glas Leitir that
Polson had to regularly check and record. Another survey that had important
implications for woodland restoration was a preliminary soil survey of the
Reserve by the Macaulay Institute for Soil Research. A finding of this survey was
the much greater depth of soils, characteristic of pinewood, actually found within

the open pinewood when compared to those outwith. Once again this raised the question as to the suitability and condition of the soils no longer under woodland for natural regeneration. Had these soils degenerated from pinewood forest soils and if so how would it be possible to know the original extent of the natural woodland? And if the soils were no longer suitable for natural regeneration how could there be an extension of the pinewood, if that was what was wanted? It was recognised, however, that there were many areas below the tree line on Beinn Eighe that had never supported woodland – for example, where the peat was very shallow with mainly deer grass and purple moor grass or where there was impeded drainage and bog.

One of those bogs in the woodland had become known as 'Tansley's bog'. This stemmed from Tansley's pre-war visit when he first described Coille na Glas Leitir. He had come across a raised bog which he described thus in his *British Isles and their Vegetation* (1939): 'The only available description of a Scottish raised bog is that of a small but very perfect example completely enclosed by native pinewood on the south-western side of Loch Maree in Ross-shire ... This is developed on a terrace of the hillside, and is only about 150 m long by 70 m wide and oval-oblong in shape ... It appears to be quite untouched and shows the typical features of such a bog very well indeed.' A raised bog is one whose surface, through the growth of peat, is above the level of its surroundings. This little bog is such a fragile site that to ensure its long-term conservation all research and study of it is strictly controlled. Subsequently, however, it has generally been agreed among plant ecologists that it is *not* a raised bog – even experts can be wrong!

There were various other surveys carried out to complete the base line of the physiography and natural history of Beinn Eighe. For example, in 1953 work began on producing a large-scale contoured map of the Reserve, vital for planning and recording, while work on the fungi and invertebrates continued throughout the 1950s and into the 1960s.

A health check on Coille na Glas Leitir

Of all the surveys in the years 1952–3, however, that by McVean was undoubtedly the most significant, as far as the original interest of the Reserve is concerned. His research established the groundwork for restoration of native woodland and the reasons behind the present location and state of most of the relic Scottish pinewoods, including Coille na Glas Leitir itself. McVean carried out several transects through both the felled and unfelled woodland, ageing the trees and drawing up a composite picture of its age structure.

From Fig 5 it can be seen that the wood did not exhibit the classic healthy population curve from numerous seedlings at the left, through to a few very old trees on the right. Instead, there have been three peaks of regeneration in Coille na Glas Leitir: the pioneer peak at around 1760, the second at 1850 and the third around 1890. McVean also found evidence of one- to two-year-old seedlings

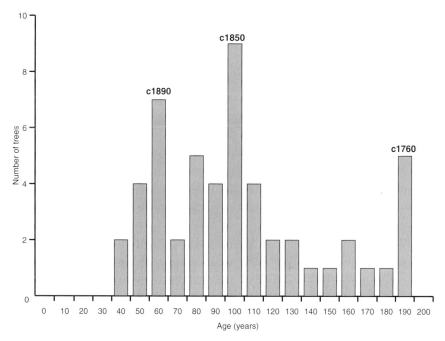

Fig 5 **Composite histogram of age composition of Coille na Glas Leitir. D. McVean 1953.**

within the woodland and some young trees and saplings mainly on the outskirts at the west end of the woodland which, he said, possibly represented a fourth regeneration peak around 1935. A large gap in the presence of seedlings to the last peak at around seventy years ago is common in pinewoods throughout Scotland. Regeneration of our native Caledonian pine wood, he added, 'on a significant scale appears to have stopped in the late 19th century'.

It was McVean who observed that the oldest trees in the wood are large, heavy-crowned trees that have their roots in a charcoal layer in the soil. This, he suggested, indicated that they became established after a major fire and grew well spaced, in open ground and not within an existing woodland. He then went on to observe that in the natural pinewood situation after a forest fire, there is a ten-year window of opportunity for tree regeneration between the fire and heather recovery. If pine seedlings are not above the heather by then the conditions for germination and growth become unfavourable and the next pulse of natural regeneration must await the next fire or other form of widespread ground disturbance, for example catastrophic wind throw.

McVean then examined the vegetation within the woodland and went on to consider why, apart from the grazing impact, there had been a lack of regeneration. Principally, as had already been suggested, it was because of the presence of a spongy layer of moss that was preventing germination and the establishment of pine seed. Natural forest fires in the past would have destroyed this mat of mosses, but today, perhaps because of the climate, the wet northern

Coille na Glas Leitir
with Loch Maree
and Slioch
in the background.
Photo: SNH

slopes – on which survive Coille na Glas Leitir and many of Scotland's remaining native pinewoods – are so damp and mossy that fires are checked. On the other hand, on south-facing slopes in Scotland where there are very few remaining pinewoods, the drier climate has allowed regular muirburn to destroy most seedlings and the forests themselves. McVean went on to say that the whole of the area west of Coille na Glas Leitir showed signs of repeated burning and the replacement of heather by deer grass and purple moor-grass and that it was only on those damper slopes which have escaped fire 'that young pines show a reasonable growth rate'. The question that then arose was: if pine cannot regenerate either in the spongy moss layers within open woodland or under dense pine stands, to what degree had people's intervention upset the natural balance? Today it is generally accepted that both climate change and human management destroyed most of the original Highland forests, but there is still plenty of argument as to which was the more responsible.

Regeneration experiments at last

A glance at the early scientific research work carried out on Beinn Eighe reveals that, between 1953 and 1966, McVean produced around twenty scientific papers and reports on his research work at Beinn Eighe. Once he and Salzen had completed their initial survey work, McVean threw himself into unravelling the history of Coille na Glas Leitir and into research on other relic native pine woodland throughout Scotland. Not only was he interested in the general question of why these woodlands no longer naturally regenerated, but in the specific soil requirements of the seeds and seedlings of native tree species; in the case of Beinn Eighe these were Scots pine, birch and alder in particular. McVean's daunting task in the earliest years at Beinn Eighe was to find ways to consolidate the existing woodland at Coille na Glas Leitir by filling in the gaps and to extend that woodland across all the suitable ground on the lower slopes of Beinn Eighe.

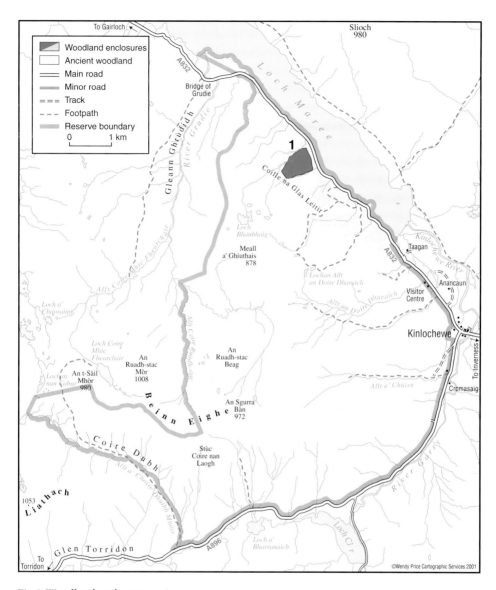

Fig 6 **Woodland enclosure no. 1.**

This was to be achieved with local seed, by the most natural and least interventionist means, and, since time and Conservancy funds were limited, it had to be done in the most rapid and least expensive way possible. After all the discussion and debate, local pine seed collection began in 1953, and in 1954 the experimental enclosure of 44 ha, the first of many, was erected in Coille na Glas Leitir. McVean then rose to the challenge, establishing a bewildering array of experiments on tree establishment within and outwith Coille na Glas Leitir in the 1950s.

McVean's first experimental trials were with broadcast seed on all main vegetation types, including those where tree growth might be expected and those where it might not. This was carried out both with and without disturbance of the ground, and with and without the addition of mineral phosphate treatment, to observe germination success and seedling survival. The early results were encouraging and it was soon found that putting down a few seeds in a very restricted area (spot sowing) was more economical than scattering (broadcasting) seed widely, relative to the amount of seed used, and it also made the measuring of the results easier. After one year McVean found that the overall success of spot sowing was just 25 per cent, with most damage caused by rodents, water logging and the feet of deer, in that order of importance. Transplanting of 5–10 year old trees was also tried and, despite the inevitable damage to their roots, around 80 per cent survived. However, they tended to be selectively browsed by deer in poor winter weather. McVean varied the experiments enormously by for example, baring the ground under scattered trees, attempting growth in wet hollows, sowing where heather had been pulled up by the roots but left *in situ* and growing seedlings in pots in various types of soil. In 1955 alone, 4000 experimental spot sowings were carried out. Scots pine was not the only subject of these experiments. He used birch and alder and to a lesser extent whin, holly, juniper, rowan and willow.

The results of this immense amount of work were a series of benchmark scientific papers on native woodland establishment and management that were to be the basis of early woodland management at Beinn Eighe and Rum National Nature Reserves, and which continue to influence native woodland management at many other places in Scotland to this day. Of several published in 1956 one was on the establishment of Scots pine seedlings and another on the establishment of the other principal native trees: birch, rowan and alder. In particular, McVean showed that phosphate fertiliser was all important in pine establishment on certain peat types and that this operated through transference of the phosphate in the soil to the seedling by a mycorrhizal (fungus) infection of the seedling roots.

In the same year, possibly at the request of Dr Joe Eggeling – who had recently been appointed Conservation Officer for Scotland and who was a forester and naturalist formerly working in Africa – McVean wrote a paper entitled 'Highland Pine Forests: Methods of Regeneration'. This was presented at the Scientific Policy Committee's meeting in January 1957 and was further discussed at the Scottish Committee later the same month. In the paper he admitted that restoring the wood by unaided natural regeneration alone was proving very difficult. This paper is of great interest as it was one of the first guides to native pine woodland establishment using different age and species groups without intensive ground treatment. At this point in his research he was beginning the last year of a five-year programme of experiments.

McVean had established beyond any doubt that promoting natural regeneration within Coille na Glas Leitir by minimal intervention methods, in other words sowing seed or hand planting if that failed, was going to take many, many years. On the surface, this was the future official Conservancy woodland restoration management policy at Beinn Eighe, but underneath there was a vein of pessimism and doubt, well summarised by the Director General, Nicholson, in the report of a visit in 1961: 'In the early days of the Conservancy, the management of Beinn Eighe was perhaps the most acutely controversial of all problems, and even when the first outlines of the Management and Research plan were adopted, there was ample room for doubt and pessimism about the possibility of salvaging this battered relic of the Caledonian forest.' This pessimism and doubt would surface in the years following the production of the first Management Plan in 1957. For the moment minimum interference methods of regeneration through research and experiment carried the day. But not everyone had the pure ecologist's patience. This was, after all, the first National Nature Reserve and it was subject to pressures from both within and outwith the organisation for demonstrable results after several years of nature conservation management.

McVean's research could be said to have been 'applied', in that he was looking for the optimal method of encouraging woodland regeneration. However, because of its great width of experimentation it was probably also regarded by some as 'pure' research, in that some of it had doubtful future application. The question of which has precedence on a Reserve, pure or applied research, has never been fully resolved. Managers of National Nature Reserves, almost by definition, are there to see results. Academic researchers on the other hand, see Reserves as the most secure places to carry out pure research, especially long-term, whose application, if any, they cannot predict. On Beinn Eighe at this juncture there was a growing feeling of uncertainty of methods being used to encourage regeneration on the Reserve as there was little to show for it.

The Warden and the Director's gooseberries

Those early years must have been an exhausting, confusing and often frustrating time for Polson. The accommodation he and his wife had been given at Anancaun in 1952 still had no mains electricity or piped water. Major repairs to Anancaun and the other farm buildings, notably the adaptation of one into a hostel for visiting staff, did not take place until the following year, when its purchase and that of the adjacent small-holding of Taagan were completed. The purchase of the latter property was important to the Conservancy since its tenant had sheep grazing rights on part of the Reserve, which the Conservancy later brought under its control prior to the resale of the croft. Like all out-posted staff to this day, Polson could never have known exactly what was going on at the centre and he would have heard all sorts of versions of events from the many staff that visited the Reserve. In addition, it could not have been entirely clear to him from whom he should take orders with so many different people arriving and demanding his time. His duties were many, including supplying researchers with directions,

regular rain gauge recording, trap inspections, dealing with campers and their fires, handling local complaints of marauding deer, and fielding the demands of land agents, administrators and Berry himself. However, his principal duty was the monitoring and management of the red deer.

Polson was employed from the beginning very much as a keeper and head stalker, a role with which he was familiar. Making the transition to Warden of a nature reserve took a few years, because at first neither he nor anyone else knew what a warden should be doing. Managing the deer meant he had to spend a considerable time on the hill gauging the size of the population and its seasonal movements as well as carrying out an annual deer cull. Then there were regular night patrols for deer poachers, a duty he took very seriously, and other responsibilities expected of gamekeepers in similar positions on Scottish estates, such as rabbit and fox control. Even after two years in post he still did not understand why muirburn was not part of Conservancy policy. It must have been very difficult for him to understand his new Director General when, on a visit in 1953, Nicholson questioned the scientific justification for Conservancy staff interfering with wildlife on a nature reserve by controlling 'pests'. Nicholson was concerned that continuing a culture of 'keepering' might result in the Warden controlling pine marten! Nicholson did relent, however, as far as the Anancaun and Taagan properties, off the Reserve, were concerned. It was not until the middle of 1954, three years after declaration of the Reserve, that senior Conservancy staff addressed the issue of Warden education and training.

Polson, with help from McVean, gradually became more and more responsible for the small tree nursery established at Anancaun by the latter in 1953, a few years ahead of the Rum National Nature Reserve nursery set up by McVean and Peter Wormell. This was one of the very few nurseries for native trees in Britain at the time and there was little guidance available as to how to treat the collected seed. However, it rapidly became successful and grew to a size that required almost full-time attention for most of the next fifty years, apart from a gap of seventeen years between 1970 and 1987 when a change in management policy, as we shall discover, led to its temporary closure.

The role of reserves in education had been stressed under the original purposes of National Nature Reserves, not only within formal education, but also through informal contact with the general public who might, through information, gain some understanding and enjoyment of their countryside and its wildlife. However, the early Conservancy, despite the influences of so many popularisers of natural history on its Committees, focused on research almost to the exclusion of the general public's

Jimmy Polson
recording the weather
at the Climatological station.
Photo: SNH

interest. At Beinn Eighe, by-laws were established of which the first ten (of twelve) begin with 'No person shall …' Polson, who became known as the Warden, was given the impression that part of his job was preventing the public from interfering with research and management. A history of poaching in the area and his role as gamekeeper only helped to reinforce that view. In fact it would take a few years and a new Warden before Beinn Eighe began to assume a much higher public profile.

On top of these many tasks Berry had become preoccupied with the idea that the small local population of Scotland's race of the greylag goose needed supplementing. The Scottish Committee approved this idea in January 1957, probably because Berry was Director, but also possibly because he knew a man in

Berry's greylag geese
(gooseberries)
in enclosure at Anancaun.
Photo: SNH

Fife, Tom Spence at Newburgh, who could provide the initial stock for free. The only problem was where to establish this flock. In August 1957 Beinn Eighe, with its own small population on Loch Maree, was chosen. These captive geese had to be looked after and it was hoped that they would breed and that young, when fledged, would then leave and supplement the wild population. Polson must have had a busy time simply deciding his priorities.

The first consignment of twelve greylag geese arrived at Anancaun in the spring of 1958. They were put in a pen and fed daily with grain and potatoes. From the very beginning there were problems, for example in August of that year a flood damaged the fence and two escaped. In November, while Polson was on leave, three were killed by a fox and then two more after he returned, so that by the end of the year there were only five left. In the following spring three more left, hopefully to join the wild population, and then there were two. These left in April and then there was none. A couple of years later Polson notes that there were around fifteen on Loch Maree and in the spring of 1960, while observing the wild geese on the loch he recognised three as being ones that had been brought into Anancaun. The project continued and in that spring Berry arrived with six more. This was very much Berry's project and he regularly enquired from his office as to how it was going. With visitors at Anancaun he used to tell a little joke against himself regarding his *gooseberries*. A member of staff recalls a European visitor struggling to understand the joke.

The 1960 Annual Progress Report acknowledged this work by adding a secondary objective to the 1957 MP, that there should be: 'the encouragement of the Scottish race of the greylag goose as a breeding species in the Loch Maree district …'

By August of 1960 Anancaun was in danger of becoming a wildfowl sanctuary with, in addition to the greylag, a pinkfoot goose (from a neighbour), mallard and shelduck. Polson himself was becoming very attached to his geese and comments when four young greylag he had raised flew off with a wild flock flying overhead: 'I was really very surprised and disappointed that the reared birds being so tame left here so readily, as they used to feed from my hand and indeed followed me in the evenings when I used to set off to collect the cows.' Numbers were now back to two. Alas, in December, a young goose that used to fly in and visit, possibly a previously raised one, hit the high-tension wires and was killed. By the following year, 1961, six more geese had been brought in and the saga continued. The winter of 1963–4, however, proved to be the nail in their coffin, or fox in their enclosure. In December a fox got two leaving four and in January he called again and as Dick Balharry (the new Warden in 1962) reported 'one more pinioned bird met its fate'. Again in March the fox came back leaving only one as the other un-pinioned one 'left presumably for safer quarters'. Finally the last record for grey-lag at Anancaun appears at the end of 1965: 'The bird missing from the enclosure has formally been dealt with'. There is no more mention of grey-lag at Anancaun, nor an explanation of what 'formally' actually meant. The epilogue to the story is that by June 1964 it appeared that the Loch Maree greylag population had expanded its nesting area with six broods in total, four of which were now at Taagan, nearer the head of Loch Maree, where they still breed today. Whether or not there is a connection between the years of effort and the expansion of the wild greylag population we will never know. However, it should be added that in the year 2000 there were still approximately the same number of native greylag geese breeding on Loch Maree as there were at the beginning.

Coire Ruadh Stac
and the ridge to the summit.
Photo: J. MacPherson / SNH

5 Achieving the ideal 1957–61

> It is the most difficult ground that could possibly have been chosen for experiments in the re-establishment of forest and scrub cover (much of it is unplantable in the silvicultural sense) and is thus a challenge to conservation research.'
>
> Beinn Eighe Management Plan, 1957

The first Management Plan

McVean's pessimistic paper on the outlook for natural regeneration provoked much discussion at the Scientific Policy Committee meeting in London in January 1957, particularly as to methods by which trees might be encouraged to grow in unpromising situations in the Highlands. It was generally agreed that the soils must be disrupted to allow tree roots access to the deep-lying minerals, and also that the layer of waterlogged peat must also be disrupted. Berry reported to Eggeling and McVean that, after the meeting was finished a member of the Committee, Sir Basil Neven Spence, had suggested using 'Camouflets', devices used by sappers to make subterranean explosions, to blow holes which could subsequently be easily drained. They gently dismissed the idea, McVean pointing out that it was actually waterlogged drift (material dropped by glaciers) that was the problem, adding: 'Why explosives rather than ploughing?'

Pearsall sounded a note of caution: apart from the proposed area south of Cromasaig in Glen Torridon to be leased to the Forestry Commission for ploughing and planting, other methods of restoring woodland should wait until McVean's experiments, by direct sowing, were completed. It was hoped that this, most natural form of regeneration would replace planting and that there would be no need for intensive management methods. The Committee agreed that the regeneration experiments should continue, but betrayed signs of impatience with results, suggesting that it would be necessary to extend the treatments so that fairly soon there might be, not simply seedlings, but actual trees on the ground.

In the middle of this process of discussion as to the future of woodland management, in July 1957, Dr J Morton Boyd was appointed the Assistant Conservation Officer for North-West Scotland. Boyd had just completed his PhD study, on the ecology of the machair on Tiree, under Yonge, with a Conservancy studentship grant. Up to now McVean had been directly responsible for the Reserve under Berry. Then Berry devolved responsibility for all the Scottish Reserves to Eggeling, who six years after the declaration of the Reserve handed responsibility over to Boyd. Boyd was not only an ecologist, but a man who had a wide field of interest in Scottish natural history and culture and – what is most important – who believed in National Nature Reserves and who championed Beinn Eighe and several others through good times and bad. Boyd had a deep belief in his own role as a conservationist, which enthused his staff through nearly thirty years in the Conservancy, latterly as its Scottish Director. Recalling his first visit to Beinn Eighe in 1957 many years later he said: 'At my feet was the magnificent country for which I had been called from childhood – not simply to a job, but to the personal care of the land I loved – like Keats I saw that wide expanse in a new light, and felt that wild surmise of new discovery. Could I enshrine with my soul the spirit of this serene country, equal the task of discovering and sharing its secrets, have intellect enough to understand it, and tell of it to others?' (Foreword to the *Nature Conservancy Council for Scotland in 1991*).

McVean had devoted a great deal of energy and expertise to the regeneration of the woodland and would continue to do so for several more years, but from now on that work would have to take its place among other priorities for the Reserve. At the same time it was decided that Polson, who now had the policing aspect of the job under control, should give more of his time to conservation work.

This was a transition phase in Conservancy culture as the 'conservation' or 'regional' staff began to take control of site management away from 'research' staff. The former were practical conservation managers who had to take into account many outside factors, such as the public, other land managers and owners on Sites of Special Scientific Interest, as well as the costs of conservation projects, and who had to be prepared to compromise to achieve their aims. The latter tended to have an academic bent and were generally more concerned with achieving the ideal. Such different attitudes were bound to lead to conflict.

Appropriately, in the very early months of 1957 it was McVean, so knowledgeable about Beinn Eighe, who began drafting Beinn Eighe's first Management Plan, to which the Conservancy's Land Agent, John Arbuthnott, and Boyd both contributed before it was finalised that autumn. The 1957 Management Plan reasserted the original reason for the Reserve's establishment and, as a result of the many surveys carried out in the interim, identified further features of conservation value: 'The tectonics and general geological interest of the area are also considered to be outstanding ... In addition, the area ... presents a wide range of forest, moorland and montane (mountain) habitats suitable for ecological research.'

Subsequent exploration revealed a more diverse flora than was at first suspected, and fascinating soil and vegetation contrasts resulting from the juxtaposition of the hard quartzite and lime-rich rocks. The plant-rich moss heath on the summit of Ruadh Stac Beag (*little red steep hill*) and the prostrate juniper of the quartzite moraine between Meall a' Ghiuthais and the foot of Beinn Eighe itself, were found to be the finest examples of these types of plant community in the country.

The Objects of Management, set down for the first time, confirmed the fairly narrow view of the purposes of National Nature Reserves: 'to maintain this area as a field laboratory for the continuous ecological study of the forest, moorland and montane habitats which it contains'. The chief ends to which studies were to be directed were: 'the re-creation of natural climax forest from the existing' and 'the diversification of the Reserve by afforestation'.

There was no indication in this plan, according to McVean, later, that any of the woodland to be restored or extended, either within or outwith Coille na Glas Leitir, would be achieved by commercial forestry methods such as ploughing and draining, except perhaps in very limited areas. The terms 'afforestation' and 'normal planting methods' used in the MP appear to refer to a now almost standardised spot sowing and hand planting established at Beinn Eighe. However, the very looseness of the terminology opened the way to later reinterpretation.

Diversification and the Forestry Commission

By the time of the appearance of the Management Plan in late 1957, some 3000 one- and two-year-old pine transplants had been set out and more than 9000 spot sowings made in the first experimental enclosure in Coille na Glas Leitir, only a small proportion of which survived. It is clear from the Management Plan that the main focus of botanical research should continue to be that of Scots pine itself and establishment of saplings. It was planned to complete a mosaic of planting and spot sowing of this first enclosure in five years time with pine and a little oak. In addition, it was proposed to lease a small area by Aultroy to the Forestry Commission to plant a 'diversification' enclosure and finally, to erect and plant a further two such enclosures over the next five years at the southern tip of the Reserve.

These 'diversification' enclosures, variously also termed by Boyd in 1958 'amenity' and 'psychological', could equally have been termed 'propaganda' plots. They were not part of the three aims of the Reserve, but were to be planted for other purposes on vegetation much modified by agriculture by the roadside. The amenity element was simply to create 'woodland' on fields where it had once existed. The psychological element appeared to be for the benefit of Polson, who wanted to feel that after five years he was both actually achieving something *and* being seen to be achieving something. The propaganda element was to demonstrate to the public and the local community that the Conservancy *was* achieving something. In his book *The Song of the Sandpiper* (1999) Boyd says of Polson and of the conflict in the latter's mind between conservation practices and traditional Highland estate management, 'When I arrived, there was stalemate and the warden, Polson, was at his wits' end in knowing what to do. In seven years the only significant step had been the fencing of a 100 acre deer exclosure in the native pine wood … Polson … could not understand the laissez-faire policy; nor

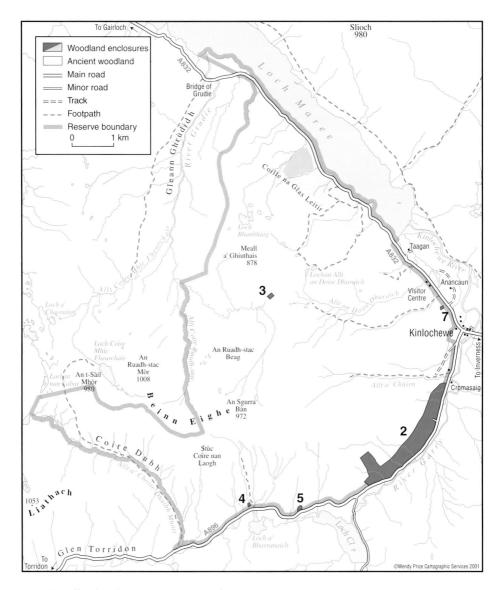

Fig 7 **Woodland enclosures nos. 2, 4, 5 and 7.**

could he abide the sight of boggy ground and took a disproportionate delight in digging small drainage schemes.'

Of the three small 'diversification' enclosures erected between 1958 and 1960, one was sited in an old, walled sheep-fank at the western end of the Reserve in Glen Torridon below Carn Anthony (*Anthony's cairn*). Coincidentally, when this was extended in 1970, one of the Beinn Eighe staff involved was Edwin Cross, the grand-nephew of Murdo Cross, whose sheep-fank was planted up and whose ruined house, abandoned less than 100 years ago, lies adjacent to the trees. All

Jimmy Polson surveys
a diversification enclosure
after ploughing.
Photo: SNH

were planted with Scots pine plus different proportions and mixtures of broadleaves.

To McVean, who had by then spent five years assiduously building up the forest nursery at Anancaun to support the needs of his vast range of experimental plantings and sowings, and who had, time and again, made it plain that re-creating the 'natural' woodland was going to take a very long time, the new enclosures were a waste of time and energy. Worse, they were going to absorb the limited finance available and use up *his* carefully collected and raised seedlings.

Boyd argued that the diversification enclosures created woodland habitat where there was none before, to the benefit of woodland birds and insects and it was he who won the support of his superior, Eggeling, with the proviso that McVean's five-year programme should not suffer.

The next afforestation enclosure to be erected – of an ever-increasing number – was that of 125 ha above the road from near the Allt a' Chùirn towards Loch Clair. This was leased to the Forestry Commission in 1958 as a result of all the Commission's pressure to allow its participation in the woodland restoration experiment at Beinn Eighe. Politically, the Commission was under pressure itself to create more forest, and therefore employment, in the area, as part of its broader social remit of the time. Over the 1960–1 season, then, the Commission ploughed and planted around 10,000 Scots pines of non-local origin, 27,000 lodgepole pine and 10,000 Sitka spruce.

Globeflower
in the high level enclosure (No. 3)
on Creagan Ruadh.
Photo: D. Miller

This intrusion of commercial forestry on a National Nature Reserve is an indication of the Conservancy's lack of confidence in nature conservation principles at the time: it is impossible to imagine such a thing happening today. However, it was planned by the Conservancy that this would later be used as a 'nurse' crop, to provide the initial shelter for the native trees already spot-sown by McVean. When the objective of these exotics had been achieved in a relatively few years it was planned that they would be felled. However, as we shall see, it all took a wee bit longer than planned and the trees remained for a further forty years.

High-altitude conservation

A very different kind of enclosure was erected in 1957 around a small area above the tree line, at 430 m on fertile soil an outcrop of lime-rich rock at Creagan Ruadh (*red-brown little crag*) on Meall a' Ghiuthais. This was intended to exclude grazing and to demonstrate the resulting effect on its flower-rich community. This diverse and colourful community of tall herbs, such as the elegant globeflower and melancholy thistle, grasses, sedges and ferns, was once far more widespread at the upper limit of the tree line in Scotland, particularly where soils are enriched from a mineral-rich bedrock. The plants growing on such fertile soils, in contrast to the tough and struggling plants on the surrounding poor sandstone and quartzite soils, are unfortunately very nutritious and therefore very attractive to grazing animals. Except where out of reach on ledges, these communities have generally been grazed to the level of short grassland by red deer, sheep and mountain hare. In 1957, this example represented one of the first of this type of community to be fenced in Scotland and there was great interest in whether it would recover, or whether coarse grasses might come to dominate in the absence of grazing.

The main problems with enclosing the site at Creagan Ruadh, as with most such examples of grazed tall herbs in Scotland, are the logistics of access and the high maintenance costs due to exposure. The communities are usually well beyond existing tracks and on rugged ground, often beneath eroding crags. Polson, however, literally rose to the challenge by arranging for the fencing materials to be transported to the site by helicopter, setting an example to be followed by many Wardens to come. The Conservancy Land Agent at the time, Arbuthnott, like all good Land Agents, was much concerned at the possible cost implications. The London office penpushers, from their Belgrave Square perspective, were also quick to spot an unauthorised and radical gamble, demanding explanation and justification by return for the use of such sophisticated methods of transport. Even they had to agree, however, that at a total cost of £27, it had been a pretty good bargain. And it still looked like a bargain in 1998/9, when the enclosure was re-fenced at a cost of £3000.

Forty years on, the results of the protection of this ancient native plant community are spectacular and well worth a visit. Like Coille na Glas Leitir on the lower moorland, the little red-brown crag is an island of diversity in a sea of poverty. If the fence were to be removed at present deer densities, the luxuriant vegetation within would quickly be reduced to the level of the surrounding grassland. The experiment is a startling illustration of the productive and aesthetic potential of not just Creag Ruadh itself, but of the several other lime-rich outcrops and flushes on the Reserve. For example, on the Mountain Trail above Coille na Glas Leitir there is an ungrazed, lime-rich crag, rich in flowering plants, below which a grassland flushed with lime provides a traditional deer calving area.

Momentum for change

Over the Reserve's first half-century, the Conservancy went through four different stages in its search for the optimum woodland restoration policy. In the earliest years the initial policy was driven by its research ethos and consisted of painstaking spot sowings and random plantings with minimal ground intervention, resulting in very modest success: all of the work carried out by McVean and only a few other staff. The second stage, after seven or eight years, involved the erection of the 'diversification' enclosures. At this point the patience of some of those involved, but certainly not McVean, began to wear thin. Had more investment been made in 'assisted' regeneration research and the fence of the original experimental enclosure in Coille na Glas Leitir been more efficient at keeping out deer, the results might have been quite different. The third stage was an acceleration of planting by turning to commercial techniques in the late 1960s and the last, the result of an enforced rethink, began in the late 1980s.

In retrospect, it was probably inevitable that the influence of the proactive conservation staff would eventually overrule the research staff. These included the Warden, the Conservation Officer (Boyd), the Forestry Officer (Wallace) and more senior staff, especially Eggeling who was a forester himself. They wanted results to justify all the effort and expenditure at Beinn Eighe. As with most momentous decisions for change, this one did not happen overnight, and today, in the inevitable absence of some of the records of the time, one cannot be sure that all the elements and influences have been identified. However, the main ingredient is fairly clear – the idea of ploughing and planting by conventional forestry means had probably never been absent from some minds.

In the summer of 1960 McVean wrote a progress report on the Coille na Glas Leitir enclosure. It was very pessimistic and, in addition to noting that the regeneration 'pulse' following the wartime felling and burning was now over and that browsing damage (by roe deer mainly) had destroyed many years of his work, he concluded that '… there is now no hope of restocking the pinewood at all adequately by natural regeneration. Further fencing will have to be carried out, preferably at the east end as planned, and seed sowing and planting must be done'. McVean, of course, meant notch planting by hand with nothing more than a spade.

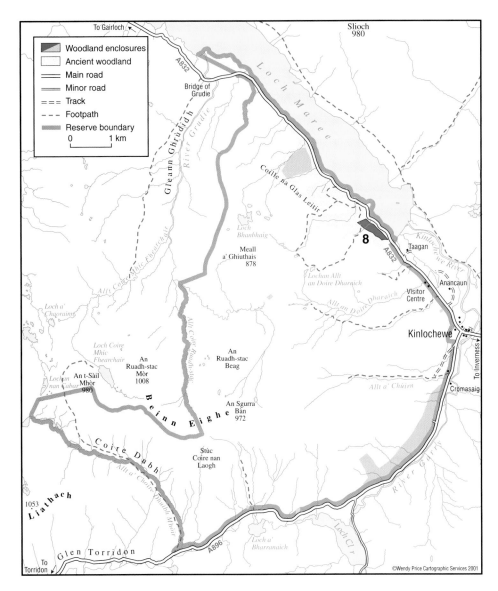

Fig 8 **Woodland enclosure no. 8.**

In September 1960 Boyd wrote to Pearsall, who had had so much influence on early management, seeking comments on a proposal for a second restoration enclosure of 16 ha to the south-east of the first in Coille na Glas Leitir. This was to be the first step in the restoration of previously felled areas within the ancient woodland remnant where natural regeneration might be expected. In his letter Boyd did not mention the possibility of ploughing and Pearsall's reply was enthusiastic: 'I have always felt that the Conservancy has failed in its duty here, so that I welcome any increase in activity.'

'Ecological' ploughing within Coille na Glas Leitir.
Photo: SNH

At the October 1961 Scottish Committee meeting it was reported that: 'Dr Eggeling said that he thought that the Conservancy might not get satisfactory results by strictly natural methods.' Is this ground preparation for a change in direction? Officially, any proposal for ploughing was to be restricted to the original experimental enclosure in Coille na Glas Leitir and the first available written evidence that ploughing might take place in the new enclosure occurs in a letter from Boyd to Wallace in November 1960: 'I am thinking now in terms of using commercial forestry methods in part of it.'

In March 1961, the proposal for ploughing was officially sanctioned by Eggeling following a visit to the site with Boyd, Wallace, McVean and Pearsall. From the beginning, Pearsall had thought time had run out for natural regeneration, but, somewhat surprisingly, he agreed to a more commercial approach. Perhaps it was no coincidence that at the same time Eggeling noted that it was not possible to plough in the experimental enclosure as any change in management there would require the permission of the Scottish Committee, several of whom had originally opposed anything other than natural regeneration and therefore might have objected – and anyhow, funds were only available for the new one. Staff were plainly bypassing the Committee. It was at this point that Eggeling informed Wallace, who had recently moved from the research branch under McVean to the position of Forestry Officer under Eggeling, that all future enclosures were to be under the control of conservation and not research staff and that he (Wallace) should see this against a 'background of the urgent need for pushing ahead with widespread afforestation on our ground at Beinn Eighe, in the Cairngorms and on Rhum'. This was surely the forester in Eggeling speaking and it was to be a major turning point in woodland restoration policy.

At this point, McVean the researcher made a plea that the Conservancy could justify this conventional forestry approach only 'by using it as a research tool, and by producing a woodland which differs appreciably in structure, composition and regeneration potential from the standard forestry plantation', echoing the concerns of Diver almost ten years earlier. However, others considered that the new enclosure was too small for his experiments. The radical or retrograde step – depending upon one's point of view – was therefore taken to plough, although it was only carried out on the 20 per cent that would not have supported trees without ploughing. Areas where there was natural regeneration were left unplanted and some 20,800 trees, six times as many trees as planted in the original enclosure were planted, by far the majority of which were Scots pine (see Appendix 1). The rate of restoration of the woodland therefore rapidly increased.

The final comment on the first ten years of woodland management came from the Director General, Nicholson, on a visit in 1961. Generally, he felt much had been achieved since the 1957 Management Plan, particularly well illustrated in the first enclosure that 'demonstrates encouragingly the possibility of natural regeneration ...' when freed from browsing and tall heather. Then he asked a critical question: is there sufficient and robust statistical data and recording on the Reserve so that the results of experimental work can be made best use of? Boyd was to take this up with McVean and Wallace and a great deal of effort, some of it in vain, was put into pegging out and mapping the experimental plots. Outwith the woodland work, the Director General was also disappointed with the 'scandal' of roadside litter and the quality of the campsite and suggested making the latter a model that the Countryside Commission might follow.

From the erection of the earliest enclosure in 1954 through to 1965, McVean continued to carry out his vast range of experimental sowings and plantings while Polson was extremely busy (until he left in 1962) assisting McVean and Wallace, supervising and supporting fence erection, carrying out work on the diversification enclosures, controlling browsing by deer, draining, weeding, planting and fertilising, and gradually taking over more of the nursery work. The next phase of planting did not begin until 1965 and the establishment of the second Management Plan, which we will pick up in the next chapter.

Early deer management

In his article 'Britain's First Nature Reserve' in *The Sphere* (Dec. 1951), Darling, in regretting somewhat that the Reserve was named Beinn Eighe, as not a lot of that mountain was actually included in the Reserve, went on to say, 'It is no criticism of the Conservancy to say that the boundary of the Reserve is not one which a biologist and geographer would have chosen. If chance should ever come, it is to be hoped that the rest of Beinn Eighe will be added to the property, and the rivers of Coire Dubh [*black corrie*], Coire Mhic Fhearchair [*corrie of the son of Farquhar*] and Glen Grudie be the boundaries. This would be a further 3000 acres of pastorally useless land, devoid of human habitation.' Darling's proposal was not pure aggrandisement; he was concerned with red deer management, for although deer are sensitive to geographical boundaries they recognise no abstract human boundary. In fact the local Gaelic name for the Reserve area *and* Grudie

Estate is Frith Cheann Loch Iù (*Kinlochewe deer forest*). With the present boundary, he noted, managing red deer numbers on the Reserve, as on almost every Highland estate in Scotland, will always have to take the interests of neighbours into account. In 1973 part of Darling's wish did come true when a Management Agreement made with the owner of Torridon Estate, The National Trust for Scotland, brought Coire Dubh within the National Nature Reserve boundary and allowed more integrated deer management.

The 'deer forest' on the Reserve was regarded, particularly by Pearsall, as just as important as Coille na Glas Leitir and therefore in the early days red deer management was based on the traditions of Highland estates. It was probably not even questioned, except by Darling. Culling was selectively carried out to remove yeld (barren) hinds, stags with poor antler formation and any beast that did not look as if it would survive the winter. This selection of animals for culling was thought to 'improve' the herd, resulting in more productive hinds and stags with more impressive antlers.

However, there was, and is, a conflict between a relatively high number of red deer and natural woodland regeneration in the absence of protective fencing, hence the enclosure approach to restoration of woodland at Beinn Eighe from the earliest days. It has to be said that there is no evidence for an increase in the deer cull in those early days to compensate for the loss of wintering ground through the erection of enclosures and there must have therefore been an inevitable increase in grazing pressure within the ancient woodland. From the beginning, nevertheless, care was taken in the location and size of the enclosures, to ensure that the deer that traditionally sheltered in the wood in the winter months would not be displaced onto agricultural ground and maraud crops as well as gardens in Kinlochewe. Inevitably, this did happen from time to time, sometimes as a result of the new fences, but it had also been happening for many years before the Reserve was established.

From Polson's observations of deer movement it was immediately apparent that there was regular and often considerable movement of animals across the boundary, particularly with Grudie Estate and at Coire Dubh. The total number of deer over the period of Polson's stay, from 1953 to 1962, fluctuated from around 130 to almost 200. The range of these figures was simply a reflection of seasonal movements – an influx of stags in the winter and of hinds in the summer – and regular disturbance to counts from walkers and climbers. Outwith fences, following tradition, Polson selectively culled only a few hinds, on average one or two a year and only a handful of stags, never exceeding ten annually. However, he shot all deer found marauding in tree enclosures.

Polson's reasons for his low culls were to take account of the great amount of poaching that occurred in the 1950s and 1960s. Polson and later Wardens went regularly on poaching patrols, putting up with long hours and many sleepless nights. Poaching was taken very seriously in those days and if caught poachers were charged under the Game Licence Act of 1860. It was not until the introduction of the Reserve by-laws in 1954 that poachers could more easily be charged. On one occasion in January 1961 Polson was kept up for nine nights continuously. Often he would be called out by the local police to try and intercept poachers after lights had been seen or gunshots heard after dark. After one of the episodes he reported: 'I left the house at 11.20 pm and didn't return till 7.30 am next morning, finally finishing up the chase on the Applecross Road. We intercepted the poachers on the Lochcarron Road, having a cargo of no less than eight stags in a Ford Zephyr.' Since eight stags could not fit into the boot of a Ford Zephyr and there were three poachers, the back seat must have been rather crowded and the car must have been somewhat low on the road as it was carrying the equivalent of at least eleven grown men. A couple of months later one of those poachers was fined £10 for using a swivelled light.

A broadening of research

Polson was a countryman, well versed in gamekeeping and stalking, but not a trained naturalist. Having appointed him to the first National Nature Reserve, the Conservancy gradually encouraged him to keep clear records of all biological events or sightings of interest. Polson, however, picked up a lot from the visiting scientists, for example on nursery management from McVean and on small mammals and birds of prey from Jim Lockie. Like McVean, Lockie was on the Conservancy's research staff and carried out survey work and research at Beinn Eighe, sometimes using the Reserve as a base for wider work in the North-West Highlands. Lockie's grand-aunt, by coincidence, had once been the teacher at Kinlochewe in the 1920s and she is still remembered by several of the older residents. Lockie joined the Conservancy as the first vertebrate zoologist in Scotland and was almost immediately sent out to the Western Isles to carry out an investigation into a complaint of lamb loss to golden eagles. When that work was finished he visited Beinn Eighe and was entranced by the Scots pine and birch woodlands, and the mountains. There, he was given the freedom to select for study those elements of the fauna he felt required most attention, usually those species that conflicted most with man's economic interests. So he began a long study of pine martens, golden eagles and foxes, and later and elsewhere, the relationship between grey seals and the salmon fishery.

One of the first pieces of work he carried out in the 1950s was to make an index of the number of pine martens, based on counts of droppings with the assistance of Polson, who also assisted with other studies. At the time little was known about pine martens in Scotland, although it was suspected that the north-west was the main centre of population. Later, Lockie also studied the food of foxes and golden eagles. The latter two he studied in relation to the density and variety of prey which by the mid-twentieth century was very much less than it had been 100 years before. From the results of the study Lockie suggested that eagles in Wester Ross were seriously short of natural prey and were dependent on carrion to maintain

Pine marten
in Coille na Glas Leitir.
Photo: R. Balharry

their numbers, that deer and sheep in winter made up 40 per cent of eagle and 60 per cent of fox diet, and that deer calves and lambs (carrion and killed) were important in spring and summer. Lockie noted that there was twice as much carrion available to foxes, so not surprisingly they were twice as dense in numbers as eagles.

In the 1960s, in conjunction with Derek Ratcliffe (Conservancy's Chief Scientist's Team) and Dick Balharry (Warden after Polson), Lockie recorded the breeding success of golden eagles and took samples of their eggs for analysis. The same twenty-five eyries were examined and recorded annually, several close to Beinn Eighe, others scattered widely over Wester Ross and beyond. The survey revisited the hypothesis of Lockie and Ratcliffe (1964) that the poor breeding success of golden eagles in west Scotland had resulted directly from the effects of dieldrin (used in sheep dip) ingested from mutton carrion. The data in the earlier paper suggested an inverse relation between dieldrin levels and success in breeding. The results of the analysis of the second survey, following the banning

Derek Ratcliffe and Jim Lockie,
examining golden eagle egg,
April 1964.
Photo: R. Balharry

of dieldrin from sheep dip, showed that the proportion of golden eagle eyries in west Scotland successfully rearing young increased from 31 per cent in the period 1963–5 to 69 per cent in the period 1966–8. Concurrently, the level of dieldrin in eagles' eggs fell from 0.86 parts per million (pmm) (1963–5) to 0.34 pmm (1966–8), thus confirming their conclusions of the effects of dieldrin in their earlier paper.

The last of that small coterie of Conservancy scientists who were regular residents at Anancaun from the early 1950s to the mid-1960s was Frank Green, who had set up the meteorological station at Anancaun. Until the establishment of the Reserve there were few meteorological records for the area, but since 1953 a full range of daily weather observations has been made by staff and volunteers. In addition to the many staff visits relating to research and management there were many specialists in other fields who came to add to the ever-growing lists of species across the whole range of flora and fauna.

But Beinn Eighe was not just a base for wider eagle work on the mainland. Apart from the other North-West Scotland mainland National Nature Reserves, such as Inverpolly and Rassal, the Region under Boyd was also responsible for St Kilda, which was leased to the Conservancy in 1957 and became a Reserve in 1964. From the beginning Boyd, who had already been to St Kilda in the early 1950s, played a very important part in the survey and research carried out on that isolated archipelago, particularly the work on the Soay sheep and seabirds. He also, through his and the Conservancy's association with Fraser Darling, became involved in the grey seal work on North Rona. In the absence of any other responsible body the Conservancy took upon itself the task of trying to assess seal populations, their feeding habits and behaviour. Beinn Eighe, situated as it is in the north-west of Scotland, with its buildings and staff, proved to be an ideal base for annual expeditions to these islands. Many staff, but not all (!), looked forward to the boat trips, island camping and cliff climbing.

Climbers, campers and the Lancaster bomber

We have concentrated almost exclusively on staff efforts towards the restoration of the woodland up to now and it is time to acknowledge the many people who regularly contributed to Reserve management. The opportunity presented by the buildings purchased at Anancaun to fulfil one of the original recommendations for National Nature Reserves was taken up with enthusiasm at Beinn Eighe from the very beginning. A Scottish Committee meeting in late 1952 agreed that a Field Station should be established which would provide both accommodation and laboratory facilities for staff and visiting researchers. The modernisation and conversion of the farm buildings was completed by 1954, although electricity was not provided until 1958. For seven years, during the height of woodland regeneration experiments and initial surveys, and until kitchen facilities were added in 1961, Mrs Polson provided a catering service at the very competitive price of £1 per night.

The first additions and improvements to the Field Station were made in 1961 and came about because of an increasing demand for accommodation from universities and colleges students on field courses and by volunteer groups from schools since the mid-1950s. This had not been foreseen at the time of writing the first Management Plan in 1955, but its development brought Beinn Eighe further into the domain of public use, education and understanding and out of the original narrow vision of an almost private estate and laboratory. In the 1960 Annual Progress Report two 'secondary' objectives were added to the Reserve, one of which was 'the encouragement of … educational courses at the Anancaun Field Centre'.

Other regular visitors came for very different reasons. The 8 km ridge and range of tops that is Beinn Eighe, all the way from Sàil Mhór at the western end to Creag Dubh at the eastern end, has always been a magnet for hill walkers and climbers. That hardy breed has never been composed of the sort of people who are put off by officials or notices, private or public. Coincidentally, a surprising number of those for whom Beinn Eighe was their first mountain ridge or whose first visit to the Reserve was to the summits, were so taken with the ruggedness and beauty of the mountain that they returned later as Conservancy staff. There are a variety of access routes to the tops. From Glen Torridon, the Coire Dubh Mòr path eventually takes one through Coire Mhic Fhearchair and up to the highest point of the Beinn Eighe ridge at Ruadh Stac Mòr at 1010 m. From there it is virtually downhill all the way towards Kinlochewe via either the Allt a' Chùirn path or the pony path between Anancaun and the Visitor Centre at Aultroy. The reverse direction, however, is probably the least taxing and most gradual approach to the Beinn Eighe ridge, even if it is uphill all the way. At least from the eastern end one begins the assault on softer ground, for once above the sandstone and onto the ridge proper the broken quartzite underfoot presents a hard and unyielding surface. But, make no mistake, the Beinn Eighe ridge is only for the fit and experienced.

Grand scenery as Beinn Eighe is for the traveller on the road or majestic for those who take the time to walk the Mountain Trail up to 500 m, right at the feet of the masses that are Meall à Ghiuthais and Ruadh Stac Beag, the *pièce de résistance* of Beinn Eighe is hidden right at the north-western end of the mountain, just outwith the Reserve. In the Scottish Mountaineering Club guide to the North-West Highlands Coire Mhic Fhearchair is described as: 'a magnificent amphitheatre, where sandstone and quartzite combine to produce one of the finest expressions of mountain grandeur in the Highlands. Beyond the picture-book loch which fills the mouth of the corrie, the spectacular Triple Buttress rises from the back wall of the inner recess, an unsurpassable masterpiece of rock architecture. This ranks among the best known and finest climbing corries in Scotland.' One of the gullies between the 300 m high buttresses, known to

The saw-toothed ridge
from the air.
Photo: R. Balharry

climbers as West Central Gully, was only ascended by climbers in 1987 and has not been scaled since. Another, Far West Gully, is known to climbers for another reason. High up in its cleft lie part of the remains of a Lancaster bomber.

Many climbers and walkers in Britain owe their lives to the RAF Mountain Rescue Association (RAFMA) which was established during the Second World War for the need of the Services. This Association might well have ceased to exist in the early 1950s but for the tragic event in Coire Mhic Fhearchair. In the same atrocious winter of 1950/1 that saw John Berry unable to get north of Perthshire on his way to his first visit to Mrs Greig at Beinn Eighe – in fact, only three weeks after his abortive journey – a tragic event occurred on the mountain. In the early hours of 13 March 1951, a Lancaster from RAF Kinloss crashed into the vertical rock wall of the corrie at around 800 m altitude, killing the crew of eight.

Immediately following the crash, incredible efforts were made to recover the bodies of the crew that were scattered in one of the gullies. These attempts were made initially in appalling winter weather and they continued over several months as conditions improved. The last body was not found until August, five months after the crash. Several climbing groups and individuals, but particularly the RAF Kinloss Mountain Rescue Team, led the recovery attempts and they found their mountain expertise stretched to the limit. At the time there were many senior officers in the Services and politicians who could not see the point of the RAF having its own Mountain Rescue Service. It was said to be costly and unnecessary. The experience of recovering the remains of this particular tragedy, however, was perhaps the key event that persuaded the RAF that it *did* need a permanent and highly professional mountain rescue team in peacetime as well as war. Several other accidents and mountain rescue attempts immediately following the crash of the Lancaster only served to confirm this view. Over the decades since then the RAF Mountain Rescue Service has become a household name, especially in the Highlands. The link between Beinn Eighe and the mountain rescue team has continued to this day through the regular membership of Reserve staff in the local mountain rescue team.

Before the Reserve existed, many climbers and walkers camped where convenient by the roadside below Beinn Eighe and it was the intention of the Conservancy from the beginning that there should be an official campsite. This was partly because of the traditional fear of disturbance to stalking and the litter and hygiene problems of fly camping and fires. Although the by-laws addressed perceived camping and disturbance problems, they were also introduced as a means to combat deer poaching. Initially, informal camping was allowed on a piece of ground at the foot of the pony path, a popular route to the hill and then in 1954 this became the official campsite – probably among the first on a National Nature Reserve in Britain. By 1956, however, the number of users had trebled and the Conservancy was becoming concerned at the amount of time and effort Polson had to put in to advising and policing campers. It was decided therefore that either someone else should take responsibility for it, or the Conservancy should provide facilities, since there were no water or toilet facilities. By 1958 toilets were in place and in 1961 the site was levelled, grass seed sown and four concrete hardstandings for caravans completed. Like the campsite this was an innovation on a National Nature Reserve. In that year, his last full year, Polson mentions that, 'We have had more visitors to the Reserve this year than ever before enquiring about the "ins-and-outs" of the work being done here and of the interests of the reserve.' After the first 10 years there was no doubt that the Conservancy and Beinn Eighe National Nature Reserve were on the public map, but the new facilities for visitors were still not entirely adequate. The Regional Officer, Boyd, thought it should not be called a campsite since the ground was far too hard. The problem was, he said, that even if the campers were advised to collect bracken and grass to soften their beds, '… if one does this kind of thing in the Scottish Highlands after June, the midges arising from the "mattress" are enough to spoil a holiday!'

Now that the ground had been broken, literally as far as woodland regeneration was concerned, changes to management policy were to gather pace, hastened by the arrival of a new Warden with radical ideas, particularly in relation to the role of the public. During this next period, partly in response to a great increase in tourist traffic, the Conservancy began to reassess its public policy and to show an even greater commitment to the provision of public facilities. It also saw the beginning of the third, and in retrospect controversial, phase in woodland restoration management.

Scottish Conservation Corps
tree planting with spade only.
Photo: SNH

6 A change in direction 1962–70

> 'To achieve the primary object of re-creating a natural-type forest it has been necessary to modify the conventional methods of commercial forestry to meet the special requirements of the Conservancy.'
>
> Beinn Eighe Management Plan, 1965–9

Ecological ploughing

Dr J Morton Boyd's article, 'Conserving Nature', in the *Scottish Field* (Nov. 1961), marking the Conservancy's tenth anniversary at Beinn Eighe, was an echo of Darling's early article in *The Sphere* (1951) and a passionate restatement of the importance of Coille na Glas Leitir. It was also a vision for its future: 'The end product is envisaged as a woodland of mixed species of mixed age possessing a diverse flora and fauna of local character, and able to regenerate itself with a minimum of human interference.' This was to be achieved by: '... ecological sowing and planting where this is necessary to obtain early tree cover. In places where the natural drainage system has been blocked by human activities ... the peat is being artificially drained or ploughed ...' This does not sound like blanket ploughing and planting, regardless of the soil conditions, in the manner of the Forestry Commission, but neither does it sound like ecological planting.

Optimism for the restoration programmer had now replaced early pessimism, but it was the optimism of the fairly rapid vertical results obtained from ploughing, as much as the steady growth of trees planted on unploughed ground in Coille na Glas Leitir. Encouragement for this new approach also came from two visitors. Dr J D Ovington, forester from a Conservancy Research Station in England, reported in 1962 that: 'The progress made at Beinn Eighe is impressive and stimulating. Drainage, use of phosphate and deer fencing are clearly the answers to the problems of tree establishment.' In 1966 Carlisle added that he supported: '... the eminently sensible policy of planting trees where natural regeneration is impossible, using the correct provenance and the cultural methods most likely to give success (in this case plenty ploughing).'

This is perhaps the right moment to look a little more closely at the woodland regeneration techniques that had been used up to 1965. From the beginning McVean had experimented with spot sowing of seed in various types of vegetation and on various types of prepared ground. There had also initially been some transplanting of pine within the woodland. Then, as the nursery developed and many more seedlings became available, various other planting methods with seedlings were carried out. This evolved into planting by spade: notching the ground or overturning turfs and planting on the mound created with the addition of a handful of phosphate fertiliser. Drains were also hand dug to improve soil conditions in a number of areas. This was regarded as limited intervention.

By 1961, McVean, through almost ten years of careful experiment and observation, had established a great deal of guidance for planting a variety of different native trees and shrubs and the kind of vegetation in which to plant each of them. In order to create as natural a woodland community as possible, species were planted in natural groups. For example, on well-drained peatland Scots pine were planted with an added mixture of birch and rowan; on areas with deeper soils and bracken, oak, hazel and bird cherry were planted; and in flushes and by running water willows and alder. Unsuitable areas, such as bog and very thin soils, were intentionally left unplanted, so that the end result was a mosaic of mixed species of trees and open ground. Such was the success of this approach that it was now being applied and expanded under a similarly ambitious restoration project by Wormell on the recently acquired island National Nature Reserve of Rum. Its only drawbacks, as far as the foresters were concerned, were the length of time it took to achieve results and the limited amount of suitable ground.

In the absence of mechanical draining, this could certainly be termed 'ecological' planting. What happened next – the extension to mechanical draining and ploughing, and plantings composed of almost 90 per cent Scots pine – despite being accompanied by the other planting techniques just mentioned, cannot be called 'ecological' planting. What was actually happening was that soils were now being substantially and artificially modified by mechanical intervention so that they could support trees, perhaps where they had never been, at least since the onset of peat formation had killed them off. But 'ecological planting' is what it *was* called.

There had always been an intention to plant a diversity of native trees; unfortunately not enough broadleaf trees were being produced in the nursery. The records for 1965/6 and 1967/8 certainly bear this out. In the latter year there were 40,000 Scots pine, but only 2000 alder and small quantities of birch, rowan, holly and ash, all lined out. The preponderance of Scots pine was due simply to the fact that it was much easier to collect large amounts of pine seed and grow it successfully in the nursery than it was for the various broadleaf seeds and berries which each needed different treatment to germinate.

In 1965 Boyd, anticipating plenty of pine seedlings for planting, obtained Eggeling's approval to plan for another enclosure outwith Coille na Glas Leitir to be established in 1969. By this time the nursery had grown to the point where there were now three separate areas for seedbeds, transplants and greencrop (clovers) in rotation. As with the nurseries that had developed at Aviemore and Rum, it was becoming increasingly efficient and productive. Although Beinn Eighe staff worked in the nursery Wallace effectively ran it with the support of casual volunteers, students and regular visits from a body called the Conservation Corps. This last body brought together volunteers for specific conservation work on a formal and organised basis. In total around twenty-six volunteer-weeks went into running the nursery in 1965.

In an internal memo Boyd set out the new policy that was to be written into the 1965 Management Plan and that was to be the only written policy for woodland management for the next twenty years: '…we intend to get trees into the ground as quickly as possible by a method of ecological planting and then see what happens.' It is perhaps true to say that by now it was implicitly understood that what was being created would not, in the medium term, become a natural woodland. Instead, and in the extreme long term – over several lifetimes of conservationists – what was being created was only the progenitor of natural woodland. However, as we shall see shortly, although this divergence from the original conception of restoration of the Beinn Eighe pinewood had apparently been approved at the top, the planting of vast numbers of pine only, had not.

The Management Plan, in force between 1965–9, also reviewed the Reserve's general progress to date and confirmed and rationalised what had been taking place. It repeated the original aims of the 1957 Plan and covered some of the developing issues, setting out new objectives such as: 'the maintenance by scientific management of the red deer herd' and 'the provision and development of facilities at Anancaun for biological studies and education', and 'the development, on an experimental basis of facilities for tourists'. However, it contained no detailed rationale for the woodland regeneration programme beyond increasing the rate of cover. It also made no mention of Berry's geese.

Extensions and provenances

In 1965 another extension of tree cover began, taking it beyond the eastern periphery of Coille na Glas Leitir and onto the surrounding moorland. Ploughing accounted for almost 30 per cent (6 ha) of the enclosed ground: a greater area and proportion of the ground than previously. A further 30 per cent was left unplanted and the rest of the suitable ground planted with a mixed variety of appropriate native species. Total planting over four years consisted of some 68,660 trees, of which almost 90 per cent were Scots pine. This was treble the number of trees planted in the felled areas of Coille na Glas Leitir (see Appendix 1).

Planting on the moorland continued its eastward spread in 1969 across the Allt Sguabaig (*the little sweeping burn*). Following previous practice an increasing proportion (76 per cent) was ploughed, although once again open spaces were left as well as areas for planting on unploughed ground. Once again planting was predominantly with Scots pine. This time, however, more care was taken than in previous plantings to soften the impact of the enclosure on the landscape of otherwise open moorland.

By 1970 Boyd had become Deputy Director (Scotland) and had moved to Edinburgh. Mike Matthew, with advice from Martin Ball, now took control of the afforestation programme from Wallace. In the spring of that year, because of the great demand for pine seed, the source for a very small proportion was Glen Affric. This is the first indication that Scots pine seed was being collected beyond

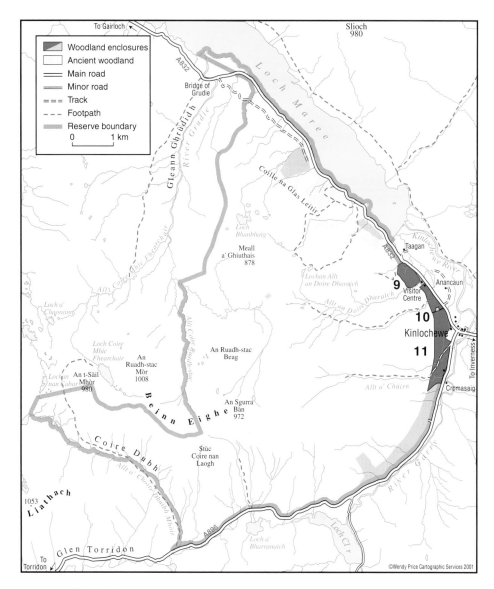

Fig 9 Woodland enclosures nos. 9, 10 and 11.

the Wester Ross area. Balharry, at the time Chief Warden for the North-West Region, had already raised a query with Niall Campbell (Regional Officer after Boyd) about the provenance from which pine seeds were being taken for planting. He was aware that some seed was coming from Shieldaig and from the Loch Maree islands, and had heard from the Forestry Commission, which owned one of the islands, that they might have planted it with pine of Baltic stock (although that is now thought to be untrue).

The attitude of the Conservancy to the issue of provenance at this point was rather ambivalent: there was concern but it was obviously not felt to be crucial. In fact, Matthew, after discussing new fence lines and enclosures with Balharry in December 1969, wrote: 'Clearly a planting programme of this size could not be carried out using Scots pine of west coast provenance only.' He went on to point out that seed from Commission non-local provenance Scots pine already planted opposite Aultroy and the Commission enclosure in Glen Torridon would regenerate on the Reserve anyway.

The issue of provenance was, however, becoming more frequently discussed, and so too was that of the increasing size of the Anancaun nursery and the staff commitment needed to keep it going. Up to now, virtually all pine seed was collected by Beinn Eighe staff and raised in the nursery before planting. By far the bulk of it was collected from local sources, if not from Coille na Glas Leitir itself. Staff numbers elsewhere in the Conservancy were expanding during this period and funds for Beinn Eighe were becoming tight, just when facilities for the public and deer management were taking up much more time than previously. As there was no prospect of more staff at Beinn Eighe it was decided to reduce the workload by switching the raising of broadleaved trees to the Rum nursery. The Commission was also approached to see if its tree nursery on the Black Isle could supply Scots pine of local Wester Ross provenance. It guaranteed a supply of 10,000–15,000 transplants from the native woodlands at Loch Maree, Shieldaig and Achnashellach, from 1971. The Anancaun nursery was therefore gradually run down from 1968 to 1971.

The concern over provenance of seed supply for the future was apparently met, but there arose some concern about possible pollen pollution of the Beinn Eighe Scots pine plantings from adjacent Forestry Commission plantations of unknown origin, never mind from the Commission's own plantings on the Reserve itself. Matthew queried the origins of these plantations with the Commission and their reply gave little reassurance: '…records show that a considerable mixture of provenances of Scots Pine have been planted in our areas adjacent to the Beinn Eighe Reserve …a good deal is definitely of east coast origin.'

In the spring of 1970, with the nursery running down and with contractors now carrying out the main plantings, Campbell, along with Boyd, Ball and Matthew, made a visit to look at progress in the overall programme. In Campbell's report of the visit to Eggeling (now Director Scotland following Berry's retirement) and others, he said, 'At the moment we are achieving a blanket coverage of pine within our afforestation plots by employing the current methods of planting and ploughing. This, of course, is not really our intention – we are supposed to be extending the natural mixed pine woodland.' It was closely planted wall-to-wall pine. Campbell envisaged that using this planting method would result in having to thin up to one in twenty pines, which would be a waste. He saw two options: either to continue with ploughing but plant Scots pine at wider spacing and intermix with birch and other native species; or not to plough, but to plant mixtures well spaced on individually treated plots. The second was close to the ecological ideal, but the first resulted in major disturbance to the soils and rows and rows of uniform pine.

There was some difference in opinion as to the alternatives among the Regional staff, but it seemed generally assumed that as Ball said, 'Current methods, ploughing and fertilising, are the only ones which will work on peaty soils. Thinning will be a necessary management process', and 'Close spacing is necessary for suppression of ground vegetation.' There was also the view that birch and pine may be successive and that it was 'unnatural' to find individual birch trees scattered in a pine forest. The strongest reaction, however, came from Eggeling: 'I was shattered to read your memo … because I had no idea that we had departed so far from the conception of ecological planting.' Eggeling, however, was concerned only about the blanket pine approach: 'Ploughing would, I think, be essential and likewise fertilisation.'

Although it seemed that 'ecological planting' was here to stay, Eggeling was concerned that the Conservancy appeared to want to establish 100 per cent tree cover far too quickly. He thought there should be a pattern of mixed age groupings and therefore a programme of planting around once every five years, perhaps for fifteen years. Matthew presented the case for the opposite view of going for rapid tree cover: 'Economies of fencing, ploughing and planting follow on this … Afforestation of the low ground is achieved relatively rapidly and more wooded ground can be opened to deer much earlier.' This, of course, depended on funds and an adequate supply of both pine and the variety of broadleaved trees that were required.

The result of Eggeling's concern and the ensuing discussion was that Boyd insisted that there must be a proper plan for the next extension of planting following past guidelines – species should be planted only in appropriate vegetation types – as laid down by Wallace. The Conservancy must not repeat the earlier mistake of planting a predominance of Scots pine. In early 1971, therefore, careful plans were drawn up for a five-year programme of ploughing and planting that would take the fenced extensions from Coille na Glas Leitir all the way to the eastern limit of the Reserve, around the elbow by Kinlochewe, and down the Glen Torridon road to the Forestry Commission enclosure. Although it was planned to plant predominantly with hardwoods, 84 per cent of the trees were once again Scots pine, the seed source for around 5000 of which was Glen Affric. There was some true ecological planting on dry knolls and wet flushes, but 60 per cent of the area was ploughed. Despite the concerns of senior management noted above, a momentum for an accelerated programme of afforestation of predominantly Scots pine appears to have established itself. This continued, between 1975 and 1979, in the shape of the last three plots, which were to be situated beyond the Commission enclosure right at the southern perimeter of the Reserve. They were to be as far as the now accepted woodland restoration policy would go, in more ways than one as we will see in the next chapter.

A different kind of Warden

Meanwhile, other important events were taking place on the Reserve. In 1962 the Reserve was extended by Management Agreement to include an area of 23 ha of ancient semi-natural woodland on the Loch Maree side of the road. Also in that year, Polson departed for the new National Nature Reserve at Inverpolly and Dick Balharry arrived as the new Warden. There were now over seventy National Nature Reserves in Britain and the Conservancy had a much better idea of the sort of people it wanted as Wardens. It was looking for people with an empathy with nature, in addition to countryside skills. Polson and Balharry were as different as chalk and cheese. Balharry arrived with all the enthusiasm of a young man given the opportunity to do just what he had always wanted. His background of gamekeeping and latterly as a stalker with the Deer Commission gave him just the experience he needed to slot into that side of the work, but he had not been in it so long that he could not view the management of deer with an open mind. He also enjoyed and made light of the hard work associated with the woodland programme. In addition, he brought with him a love of wildlife and threw himself into observing and recording, visiting the eagle eyries with Lockie, learning how to live-trap pine martens and for the first time recording encounters with wildcat on the Reserve. He wanted to share his delight in observing wildlife, however, and within a year he was to begin transforming both the thinking and the practice behind the development of facilities for the public on Beinn Eighe.

Up to 1963 a pony was hired annually to assist with deer extraction from the hill, but in 1964 Dolly, a mare from the Rum breed, became the first of several garrons to take up residence at Anancaun. Then in 1970 seven ponies arrived from the New Calgary stud in Sussex. These ponies were part of a legacy from Mrs H E K Warren, who had bequeathed around thirty-six ponies from this stud to the Conservancy. The ponies had originally been part of the Calgary stud on Mull and Mrs Warren had taken them south to conserve and improve the stud. On her death, she had hoped they might go to Rum, but that island Reserve has its own pony breed. The number of deer culled at Beinn Eighe did not require anything like as many as thirty-six ponies, so all but the seven were sold and the money raised, as well as an endowment from Mrs Warren, was used to provide a stable block at Anancaun. At the same time the Conservancy bought Glen Garry, a champion stallion from the Royal Highland Show, to complete its own breeding

Dick Balharry with Rum ponies, captive hind and faun.
Photo: Tom Weir

stock. These ponies, plus a growing number of captive deer, grazed the bottomlands at Anancaun.

Balharry built up a collection of captive animals, some to nurse, some for the benefit of the public and some, it must have seemed, just to create headaches all round. The most magnificent guest at Anancaun in the 1970s was a golden eagle called Apollo. He was taken in as an ailing youngster in May. By late June he had gained over 3 kg by careful feeding and by late July he had almost doubled his weight. A month later Apollo was feeding himself. By the following February Apollo was flying free over short distances and by April he was so active he had to be confined to barracks during the lambing season. That summer he made his debut at the Blair Atholl show and in the autumn went on to a new permanent residence at Camperdown Park by Dundee. In addition to Apollo there were also a pair of pine martens. These intelligent little animals are very hard to observe, as Lockie had found out, but Balharry found his first in the wild and it lived on in his care for seventeen years. He then went on to become the first person to successfully breed them in captivity. Balharry collected the animals to learn more about their behaviour, but senior staff in the Conservancy were not quite sure

Terry Doe deer stalking.
Photo: J. MacPherson / SNH

whether or not they should give their approval. As locals and then visitors came to hear about these animals that they rarely saw in the wild, an increasing number of people then began to arrive at Anancaun to view them.

Deer-stalking days

Just as his predecessor, Balharry had to get to grips with the deer population on the Reserve. In his first month, May 1962, at the beginning of the calving season he counted a total of 130 deer. These figures were comparable with Polson's counts. On 12 August three Red Deer Commission stalkers counted the reserve and arrived at a total of ninety-nine, far short of Balharry's count in May. Two days later on 14 August, in excellent weather, Balharry repeated the count and found a total of 171 deer. Based on his own figures he upped the annual cull level over the next decade from between eight and twelve, to around twenty-five.

However, he was concerned at the discrepancy between the three counts and commented that: 'With these figures in hand the value of a count on the Reserve is very questionable as the Reserve contains only a portion of the one-time deer forest … A deer census over a greater area including Torridon, Coulin and other neighbouring estates would be necessary to assess the movement of deer accurately.' Several years later, once he had become acquainted with the owners and stalkers on the surrounding estates, he was able to take this idea further.

Red deer, which he had stalked and watched now for ten years, were one of Balharry's particular interests. The hind calf A' Mhaighdeann was the first deer of many that were to become very much part of Anancaun over the years. She was found by Balharry beside her dead mother and carried home on his back in 1965. This was the period of intense deer research by the Conservancy, which was keen to see the management of Scotland's red deer populations move on from traditional practices entirely aimed at achieving stags with good heads for sporting purposes, to scientific management based on real knowledge of their population dynamics and behaviour. Recognising his deep interest, Boyd encouraged Balharry to work alongside the Conservancy's Deer Unit and to apply his experience to the changing needs of deer management in the wild.

Balharry then began collecting stomachs and jaws for Dr Brian Mitchell of the Conservancy's Deer Research Unit. The purpose of this was twofold. It first aimed to find out what the deer were eating on the hill and in the wood. Secondly, stalkers traditionally aged deer on the hill by features such as their condition and antler size. Balharry wanted to check this method against a more reliable feature such as tooth condition. The Deer Unit was at that time carrying out deer population, diet and behavioural research on several reserves, notably in the Cairngorms and on Rum – where the Conservancy had established the standard 1/6th level of cull necessary to maintain a deer population. Although Balharry collected samples and tagged a number of animals as part of a Conservancy programme to try and establish deer movement, Beinn Eighe was considered unsuitable for deer research due to the large fluctuation in deer numbers crossing and recrossing the boundary.

In late 1963 Boyd suggested to Balharry that they should begin to think about 'live' capture, by which he meant 'darting' deer with a tranquilliser gun after trapping to sedate them before handling. Balharry went ahead and captured four stags and a calf by enticing them into one of the enclosures at Anancaun. On his own, Balharry went on to use this live, enclosure capture technique with great effect, especially at Creag Meagaidh (*'crag of the boggy place'*) National Nature Reserve. There, with advice from John Fletcher – once a Conservancy red deer research scientist and now a deer farmer in Fife – catching pens were used to great effect in reducing deer numbers during the 1980s. The pens were a vital part of a policy aimed at restoring natural regeneration of a birch forest, without planting and *without* fencing against deer grazing. This practice of reducing deer numbers, rather than erecting fences against them, until a level is reached where reduced grazing impact allows natural regeneration of trees – demonstrated at Creag Meagaidh – is now a basic part of management policy at the RSPB Abernethy Reserve and at several National Trust for Scotland properties, such as at Mar Lodge. This practice, however, is not yet acceptable everywhere, particularly where a neighbour's deer may spend part of their time on the Reserve. There also has to be plenty of tree seed available, as at Creag Meagaidh, and suitable substrate for its germination, as at Abernethy and Mar Lodge. At Beinn Eighe, as discussed earlier, the reason for the lack of regeneration of the pinewood has been the thick layer of moss and poor soils through years of burning and lack of tree cover, as much as deer grazing.

A few years after his first live capture of deer Balharry saw another way to improve efficiency in deer management. In 1966 he took his first helicopter trip, courtesy of an Ordnance Survey team working in the area. It was May and he had planned to monitor breeding success at a golden eagle eyrie, involving a round trip on foot of 11 km, representing a whole day's work. By helicopter, Balharry arrived at the eyrie seven minutes after take-off. However, it was not only the pleasure with which he accomplished the normally arduous task that excited him, but the ease with which he was able to count and classify red deer during the flight. He at once saw the potential both for quick deer counts and for the transportation of stalkers into, and carcasses of culled animals out of, remote areas. This was a revolutionary concept and it was to take many years before it became an acceptable method of deer extraction. Later, he pioneered this extraction method at Creag Meagaidh.

Stalking is mostly very hard work in trying conditions for both man and pony. What the lay person is not aware of, for example, is the frequent need to drag a beast, perhaps after a long day's stalk in rain or sleet, from the position where it has been shot, to the roadside or a position where a pony may be able to reach it. Many former stalkers, ghillies and estate workers, including those who worked at Beinn Eighe, have not surprisingly suffered back problems in later life. However, nearly all look back with nostalgia to their days on the hill.

For anyone less than 100 per cent fit therefore, a day stalking on the hill can seem endless and exhausting but in the end, very satisfying. Osgood MacKenzie in his *A Hundred Years in the Highlands* (1921) describes in his wonderfully laconic manner a youthful adventure on Beinn Eighe, stalking and killing a stag in Coire Ruadh Stac, then catching a wild pony to carry it home. Campbell recorded an older man's long day out with Balharry in the 1960s. His record of the day is peppered with *Boys' Own* comments such as: '... set off at an extremely strenuous (to me at any rate) approach ... after a very difficult approach down the valley with a swirling wind ... our quarry had moved ...over the next ridge but one ... panting and stumbling ... a dog-trotting man will eventually catch them up ... However, there was nothing to be seen ... we split up ... I dropped and had a quick shot. Balharry fired a split second later ...' Finally, they got to the stag and, 'When the beast was gralloched we were most surprised to find only a thin strip of skin separating our two bullet holes!' The two shots fired a split second apart from different positions had passed almost through the same spot!

Trail blazing

From the establishment of Beinn Eighe as a National Nature Reserve visitor numbers *had* steadily increased. This reflected the general expansion in tourism and hill walking all over Scotland after the Second World War, when many more families were able to afford their own car. Up to the mid-1960s, apart from the campsite and caravan park, the Conservancy had dealt with the increased pressure in an *ad hoc* manner, but it was becoming increasingly obvious that it would have to develop strategies to cope with the visiting public. During Balharry's first year he was quickly made aware of the problems of litter and lack of facilities, confirmed by an article in the *Scots Magazine* by the popular writer Tom Weir, describing the road by Loch Maree as the 'litter centre' of Scotland. In the summer of 1964, therefore, Balharry and Estate Worker Andrew Christie made an all-out effort to prepare and complete a new picnic site by Loch Maree on the opposite side of the road from Coille na Glas Leitir. They managed to complete levelling of the site in the summer and in the winter they made their own picnic furniture for visitors from local wind-blown Scots pine. With no precedents to follow they sawed and fashioned tables, benches and signs on an almost 'Desperate Dan' scale from unprepared timbers. They also completed a bridge across the Allt na h-Airbhe (*burn of the boundary dyke*) by the picnic site so that the public could walk along the shore of the loch and perhaps learn something about the wildlife of the area. By the peak of the following 1965 season, when it was estimated that one tourist car per minute was passing Anancaun, the picnic-site was acclaimed a great success by visitors. However, it was so successful that it overflowed in the first year and the overspill created problems on the old informal parking sites, just as before. Two years later, therefore, the car park was doubled in size.

Many in the Conservancy were not at all convinced by the needs for, or the benefits of, these public facilities. Nature Reserves had been conceived of as places for research and nature management, perhaps places for quiet enjoyment by amateur naturalists, but not places to actually attract and inform the general public. That was what National Parks and Rangers were for, but then, of course, there were no National Parks in Scotland. Despite the lack of support Balharry pressed ahead. Norman Moore (Conservancy, England) succinctly described how such things were achieved in the organisation: 'My experience while working for the Conservancy showed me that nearly all the effective actions of that body were due to determined efforts of individual people who identified themselves with particular problems and promoted them until they had achieved their objectives' (*The Bird of Time*, 1987).

At that time the Conservancy's Interpretive and Education section, was quite small, based in England and quite remote from Beinn Eighe. In addition, the Conservancy's field staff of Wardens up to then had been recruited, by and large, from estate work, game-keeping and even the police force. Very few had the experience or training of a Ranger to welcome and provide information for visitors – the Countryside Commission for Scotland had yet to be formed. Conservancy Field staff were therefore suspicious of these new leaflets and signs, and of encouraging visits by schoolchildren to the Reserves. In 1965, however, the Conservancy contracted a firm of interpretive experts from North America to report and advise on the provisions at British National Nature Reserves. At the same time, Balharry made a study-tour of American National Parks and came back greatly impressed by their positive approach to public access, interpretation and signage. As a result of all this the 1965–9 Management Plan included a new objective: 'The Reserve must be equipped to receive an ever-growing number of visitors, ranging from those who merely want to seek general information and find a pleasant view or picnic spot to those who genuinely wish to learn.' In addition to the car park and picnic site, it was recognised that there should also be nature trails and an information centre. These concepts were considered rather radical and 'American' in those days and hence a further statement that these facilities for tourists should be 'on an experimental basis' qualified the new objective.

In 1966, two new facilities for the public were provided, one of which was a new campsite at the Taagan road end, replacing the original. The second facility, which built on the success of Balharry's picnic site, was Scotland's first nature trail, although it was not originally conceived as such. Under enthusiastic pressure from Balharry, Boyd designed a walk along the shore of Loch Maree to the west of the

The Balharry threshold sign in 1966.
Photo: R. Balharry

picnic site. Balharry, staff and volunteers worked hard to have it ready in time for its opening in April. Boyd's accompanying leaflet proved to be immensely popular and most of the first run of 450 had been distributed by May. Balharry and Boyd, however, were not satisfied by the first attempt so the following year a second trail of 1.5 km was opened following an old timber-extraction route through Coille na Glas Leitir. The leaflet for this trail concentrated on the history of the woodland and the regeneration work of the Conservancy. This trail quickly became a very popular tourist attraction and when nature trail signs replaced the picnic site signs, there was an immediate upsurge in visitor use.

The public facilities that were created at Beinn Eighe were not to be found anywhere else in Scotland. The nearest similar facilities were probably in the Peak District National Park in England. Their particular success possibly arose from the fact that they were originally conceived, constructed and written by enthusiastic naturalists. Many traditional conservationists may have seen the changes at Beinn Eighe National Nature Reserve as a bonfire of the rules, but the

The Balharry picnic furniture.
Photo: R. Balharry

more progressive saw it as a beacon. The interpretation of nature and nature conservation on Beinn Eighe in the late 1960s made it a draw for visitors and professional interpreters alike and had a huge influence on future Reserve facilities.

After all the work put into the new picnic and campsites, the weather in December 1966 wreaked havoc. It was the wettest month recorded at Beinn Eighe to date with a total of 56 cm (22 in.) of rain, 12 cm falling on one day alone. The result was severe flooding in Kinlochewe. At the picnic site by Loch Maree all the chairs and tables were either floating or submerged and the water level even reached the handrails on the footbridge leading to the nature trail, whose cairns were all washed away. Luckily, all the picnic furniture was recovered and able to be re-sited. The record was short-lived. The following March total rainfall reached 58 cm, once again making a pond out of the picnic site.

Coincident with the development of the public-friendly facilities at Beinn Eighe in the late 1960s was the establishment in 1967 under the Countryside (Scotland) Act of the Countryside Commission for Scotland, one role of which was exactly what Beinn Eighe was attempting to provide – quiet family recreation in the countryside. Although attitudes on the ground had changed, they had not at the highest levels. In its report to the Select Committee on Scottish Affairs in 1972 the Conservancy said that it felt there was no overlap between its field and that of the Countryside Commission for Scotland. It was to be another twenty-five years, until that organisation was amalgamated with the Conservancy and the public

**Working high
on the Mountain Trail
in 1970.**
Photo: SNH

access and interpretation role officially became that of Scottish Natural Heritage. A second coincidental event was European Conservation Year in 1970. This was a Europe-wide effort of governments and national nature conservation bodies to raise the profile of nature conservation that proved to be extremely successful, firmly establishing it in the public mind. The result was an increase in visitors to the country looking for facilities such as those at Beinn Eighe where European Conservation Year was celebrated by yet another new facility.

The Coille na Glas Leitir, or Woodland Trail, climbed gently through the wood to around 100 m. Very soon there was pressure from the public for a trail that would climb higher, one that might give the visitor a 'mountain' experience of this mountain reserve. The route of this proposed circular Mountain Trail of 6.5 km, rising to 550 m, took two years to survey before it was constructed and opened in 1970. It was Balharry who set the route of the trail, but it was an estate worker with a rather unusual background and unforseen skills, Lt-Col. Anderson-Bickley, retired, who carried out the survey and mapping of it. The trail was a first for Britain and was probably the first time a footpath had been constructed in such difficult terrain in the Highlands since pony paths were developed for stalking in the nineteenth century.

The scale of the achievement of this high-level, self-guided trail, from its vision, to planning and construction is incredible and can best be appreciated by taking the three- to four-hour hike up and around it. Its completion involved an immense amount of hard work and the re-establishing of traditional path-building techniques as well as the development of new ones. The result is a unique experience for visitors, who might not otherwise have ventured far off the road: it takes them from the security of the pine forest zone high up into the wildland of the mountain zone. There, the view from the plateau at the top of the Trail is one of the finest in Scotland. It looks north over the tops of the pine trees of Coille na Glas Leitir and almost the length of Loch Maree across to Slioch and the remote mountains of Letterewe.

In 1970–1 the car park opposite the path's starting point was tarmacadamed and enlarged and a catwalk constructed in a culvert under the main road. In the summer of 1971 this car park quickly filled with up to fifty cars at peak times and this was at a spot around 80 km (50 miles) beyond Inverness. Balharry was the driving force behind the provision of these new facilities for visitors at Beinn Eighe, but the achievement is shared by his staff and the many volunteers who contributed the manpower.

Volunteers and schoolboys

By the mid-1960s, a great range of groups and long-term volunteers were coming to Beinn Eighe to carry out conservation work. One group, which came regularly from 1964 to the end of the decade and then sporadically thereafter, was composed of pupils from George Watson's College in Edinburgh. Their leader over these years was the biology teacher Pat Eddington. Groups of twelve third-year boys (later, girls when the school became co-educational) aged around 14–15 were taken out of the city of Edinburgh for a fortnight in May into the wide-open spaces of the Scottish Highlands, some for the first time, to broaden their horizons and give them new experiences. Conservation work combined with some mountaineering while resident at the hostel at Anancaun and the Mountaineering Hut in Glen Torridon were an ideal mix. The boys carried out a whole range of work from phosphating the newly planted trees, to carrying gravel up the Woodland Trail. Through helping with the captive stock of animals they also got the opportunity to see many they had never seen in the flesh, such as fox, birds of prey, pine marten and deer.

One of the many pupils who came at that time was Chris Smith, who went on to a career in politics and who, from 1997 to 2001, was Minister of Culture. He climbed his first Munro while at Beinn Eighe and recalls surveying trees and measuring their growth. His first visit had such an impact on him that he returned a year or two later after he had finished his school-leaving exams. He describes the experience in his foreword to this book.

In Balharry's time through the 1960s and early 1970s, many volunteers came and went, as did several estate workers and a number of seasonal staff. David MacPherson, who left in 1964, was replaced by Andrew Christie, who in turn left in 1967 and was replaced by Edwin Cross, a local man from Kinlochewe. Cross was later to become a Warden, spending all of his working life with the Conservancy, twenty-one years of it on Beinn Eighe: he is the longest-served member of staff to date. At the same time as Cross began work, the Conservancy took on Anderson-Bickley who stayed for seven years and proved to be a great success, particularly in his care of the public facilities and the public themselves, but also through his surveying and wood carving skills.

Gairloch Conservation Unit

From the very beginnings of the Nature Reserve at Beinn Eighe it had been accepted that deer management would constitute one of the most important activities of the Warden. The problem for deer management on the Reserve is that it is only a part of the deer forest of Kinlochewe. Red deer are highly mobile, particularly stags during the autumn rut and they regularly cross estate boundaries. It is a little known fact among urban dwellers that before they are culled deer are not the legal property of anyone. Traditionally therefore, sporting estates have not co-operated with their neighbours and they are very nervous when 'their' deer cross onto Conservancy property or those of nature conservation charities. Without upsetting its neighbours therefore, the Conservancy could do only a limited amount to control deer numbers on the Reserve and so reduce grazing pressure on the regenerating Coille na Glas Leitir. In the first fifteen years of the Reserve there was only casual co-operation in deer management between it and its neighbours, which mostly consisted of helping out a neighbour if it was unable to reach its target cull.

Balharry had realised in his first season (1962) that there needed to be wider co-operation in deer counting and gradually evolved the idea over the next few years through informal discussions with Beinn Eighe's neighbours and with Boyd. By 1965 the idea had become official policy, being incorporated into the 1965–9 Management Plan with the aim of a co-operative project: '... having as its aim exchange of information and the wise management of the deer forest as a whole'.

In his book *The Song of the Sandpiper* (1999), Boyd recounts how he and Balharry discussed the idea of wider management while high on the slopes of Beinn Eighe. From their viewpoint they could see all the various forestry projects that were taking place, from the Conservancy's relatively small enclosures to the large Commission plantations. There was no co-ordination among these forestry projects or of the surrounding land, nor was there co-ordination in the management of the deer that were displaced by them. The problem was that everyone had different agendas. The Commission wanted no deer in their plantations at all, the Conservancy wanted very few, one estate wanted as much venison as possible, while others were sporting estates wanting a maximum number of stags with large antlers and lots of hinds to produce them.

Kinlochewe Deer Forest is itself part of a larger geographical unit – one of the many jigsaw pieces of north-west Scotland – that lies between Loch Torridon, Glen Torridon, Loch Maree and the sea, an area of approximately 34,600 ha. Within this area the red deer population is fairly discrete, with little immigration

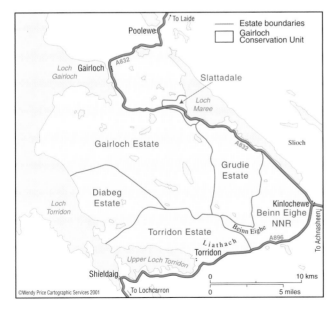

Fig 10 **Gairloch Conservation Unit.**

or emigration across its natural borders: an ideal unit within which to seek management co-operation. While Balharry continued informal lobbying of the neighbouring estates as far as deer management was concerned, Boyd took a wider view of co-operative management. In June 1966 he sought help from John Miles (Conservancy research scientist) on the feasibility of a land-use survey of the area. This was intended to help identify present and potential future land use and would form the basis for co-ordinated and strategic land planning. In September 1966, Boyd then went on to hold meetings in Inverness with the Ross-shire County Development Officer and Planning Officer, the Forestry Commission's Conservator for the area and the Research and Planning Officer of the Highlands and Islands Development Board.

Boyd explained his perception of the need for co-ordination in the main land uses of the North West Highlands, namely agriculture, forestry, sheep farming, tourism and deer management and he reported, 'It appeared that Professor Grieve [Chairman HIDB] and himself [the un-named Research & Planning Officer, HIDB] were thinking along similar lines to myself … of developing the idea of a multiple resource land-use unit with high wildlife and tourist potentials as a distinct form of land-use planning unit.'

Meanwhile, Balharry, who was more concerned with deer management, reported that the owners of two of the estates within the area were interested in getting together with the Conservancy and the other estates to discuss deer management. In February 1967 therefore, Balharry called the first meeting of the Gairloch Conservation Unit, consisting of the owners of Flowerdale, Grudie, Shieldaig, Diabeg, Torridon and, of course, Beinn Eighe. Three months later, in May 1967, Torridon came into the hands of The National Trust for Scotland and from then on its Ranger, Lee MacNally attended and contributed to the Gairloch Conservation Unit meetings. At this first meeting it was agreed by all the owners to carry out a co-ordinated deer count of the whole area and one day in early March twenty counters set out to cover an area of 350 sq km in one of the first large-scale deer counts in Scotland. The weather was not good; at the western end of the area it was so appalling that counters there had to abandon the attempt in the face of a gale and driving rain. However, after three more days of effort the first count totalling 1563 deer was completed.

Following the count there was some informal discussion on deer management, such as the ideal sex ratio, benefits to the deer and drawbacks for the environment of artificial feeding and the merits and demerits of culling of milk hinds (with calf) as opposed to the traditional yeld (barren) hinds only cull. Within two years the Conservancy, mainly through Balharry, had introduced the one-sixth cull level. The rationale for the size of the cull within the Gairloch Conservation Unit was based for the first time on the total area of grazings, the number of sheep, an accepted stag ratio of one per 400 ha and a sex ratio of two hinds to one stag. This latter ratio was, at that time, considered the optimum for producing a deer population that gave an adequate number of stags for sport stalking and hinds, both for venison and to produce the required number of stags. The group accepted the rationale and agreed to implement the required culls.

The benefit of the group approach became immediately apparent when deer did not move as predicted and the owner of one estate was then able to alter the level of its cull to compensate for the lack of, or extra, deer culled on its neighbour's ground. There was also co-operation in combating the problem of poaching which was prolific in some years. Other new ideas were introduced, such as not culling good yeld hinds for venison, but leaving them to breed the following year and the selection of poor immature stags for culling. The regular meetings also gave the Conservancy the opportunity to explain its own forestry and deer management policies. Despite many occasions when poor weather prevented culling or agreed selection criteria were not adhered to, by the time of writing in 2001 the deer population in the area showed no increase over 1967 levels in contrast to many other parts of the Highlands where overall numbers are still going up. Boyd's more ambitious plans for co-operative management of other natural resources, however, came to naught, but the Gairloch Conservation Unit was the first Deer Management Groups of many that today cover the red deer range in Scotland.

HRH Princess Margaret
crossing footbidge
with Dick Balharry after
opening the Mountain Trail
in 1970.
Photo: SNH

7 What is a natural woodland? 1971–79

'The most successful essays in natural woodland re-establishment at Beinn Eighe as I see them now are the unplanted ... and the planted areas (of Coille na Glas Leitir) which have been "written off" and are showing some first signs of becoming a finely varied area of open woodland with beautifully varied stands of pine ...'

Dr J. Morton Boyd, 1978

Cottage to visitor centre

So successful were the Woodland and Mountain Trails, the picnic and camping sites, and Balharry's animal collection in attracting the public that in May 1970 staff had to put up a sign at the Anancaun road end to direct the public to the Information Centre in Kinlochewe, simply in order to get some peace to carry out their day-to-day work. Beinn Eighe and its tourist facilities had now become a very important asset to Wester Ross, helping to draw tourists to the hotels, B&Bs, shops and cafés.

In the same month HRH Princess Margaret opened the Mountain Trail as part of the celebration of European Conservation Year. This involved a reception and meal held at a local hotel and then the party moved to the picnic site before going on to the start of the Trail. There, pupils from George Watson's College who were working on the repair of the lower Trail formed up as a guard of honour along with a visiting group of Scouts and a group from the Scottish Pioneer Corps of the Army. Uncomfortable in his formal clothes, Balharry quickly changed into his field clothes in the caravan he had placed there earlier for that very purpose. When the point came for him to hand the scissors to Her Royal Highness to cut the tape he realised he had left them in his formal clothes in the caravan. Standing next to him was Dr Boyd's wife, Winifred. Out of the side of his mouth Balharry asked her if she had a pair of scissors in her handbag. Luckily she had a tiny pair and these were handed to Princess Margaret, who managed with a struggle to cut the tape.

The trails rapidly became extremely popular and by 1973 it was estimated that 13,000 people used the Woodland Trail and some 5000 the Mountain Trail. In 1983, Bill Taylor (then Warden) commented that the Mountain Trail was so popular, compared to anything else he had been involved in that it was the only time in his career visitors to a Reserve had sought him out to thank him, and the Conservancy, for the unique experience they had just had.

Concurrent with the provision of nature trails was the development of the old cottage at Aultroy as an Information Centre. The message that the display

Beinn Eighe NNR Visitor
Centre, formerly known as
Aultroy Visitor Centre.
Photo: SNH

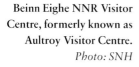

originally provided to the visiting public in the early 1970s was primarily the link between the physical geography of the North West Highlands, wildlife, land use and the need for conservation and visitor management, as demonstrated by the Gairloch Conservation Unit. The physical geography of the area was realistically illustrated by an ambitious six inch to the mile, three-dimensional model made up of three 8ft by 4ft sections of polystyrene. Balharry parcelled out the Herculean task of its construction to three groups. He supervised the building of one section; another was done by the pupils of Dollar Academy and the third by boys at the Young Offenders Institution at Polmont from which small groups came annually for a time for conservation work. Each of the three sections was then brought back together at Beinn Eighe where they were carefully united before being proudly displayed at the Aultroy Visitor Centre.

Princess Margaret must have enjoyed her visit to open the Mountain Trail in 1970 for she returned in September 1976 to visit the Aultroy Visitor Centre, which had been opened in 1974. A requirement of planning permission for Aultroy was

*Inside the Visitor Centre
prior to
most recent upgrade.
Photo: N. Benvie / SNH*

the provision of toilets, which proved an attraction in their own right in this remote area where public facilities were few. Tour buses soon discovered their location and it has been suggested that this was one of the reasons that visitor numbers to Aultroy grew rapidly from the initial 3400 in 1974 to around 7250 by 1976. That is unfair though, the model was an unusual facility in Wester Ross that gave visitors a unique impression of the physical geography of the area. Likewise, around 600 Mountain Trail and more than 1000 Coille na Glas Leitir leaflets were purchased by eager walkers, the new car park was regularly filled to capacity with fifty cars and the camp site with twenty-six tents. Through dint of many years of effort, the Nature Trails and the seasonal Information Centre at Aultroy were successfully channelling visitor pressure to the Reserve and to Anancaun.

Financial constraints in the Conservancy in the late 1970s and early 1980s almost caused the closure of the Visitor Centre but with the help of Highland Regional Council it survived. Minor amendments were made to the internal display over time but it was not until the late 1980s, as we shall see in a later chapter, that the emphasis of the display shifted from the Gairloch Conservation Unit and wider environment back to the Reserve. The earliest Nature Trail leaflets of the early 1970s, on the other hand, did inform visitors about the wildlife that would be seen and about the Conservancy's work on the restoration of the native pinewood.

Inspired Wardens and volunteers

The Trails were big and expensive commitments and both John Theaker (Warden, 1971–3) and Andrew Campbell (then a volunteer) were involved in various cost-cutting schemes to meet the needs of maintenance and repair. For example, the former was involved with an Army group who built a bridge over the burn by the car park, while the latter, at a time of high unemployment, became foreman of a proposed squad of four young men under a, none too successful, Government Manpower Services Scheme to repair the Mountain Trail. Working half-way up a mountain was obviously not the training they were looking for: only two of the four turned up on the first day and one of these only lasted a week. Pupils from George Watson's College and volunteers from the Conservation Corps also assisted Campbell.

The field station at Anancaun, which initially had consisted of accommodation and laboratory facilities for visiting Conservancy research staff, such as McVean and Lockie, was also being used by 1960 by universities and colleges for field courses. Some groups, such as Scouts and the Conservation Corps and occasionally school groups, became quite involved in practical work on the Reserve, from weeding in the nursery, to planting trees and creating and maintaining footpaths among many more mundane tasks. One of the aims of the 1965–9 Management Plan was that there should be: 'The development of the Anancaun Field Station as a centre for education out-of-doors.' This was an

Walkers
on the Mountain Trail
in 2000.
Photo: J. MacPherson / SNH

ambitious plan to run residential wildlife conservation courses at Beinn Eighe led by the Warden and other Conservancy specialist staff as needed. This would have demanded the regular commitment of both Reserve and Regional staff and possibly some specialists from headquarters, for lecturing and demonstration. Unfortunately, because of limited funds and other staff priorities, this idea came to nothing. Nevertheless, many visiting groups continued to use the hostel and laboratory at Anancaun through the summer seasons of the 1960s and 1970s; the Warden gave many illustrated talks to the visiting groups, to the public, schools, individuals and the Conservation Corps who turned up in numbers every year to assist in all the tasks. Anancaun remained a place of hectic activity in the summer months.

In 1973, funds were at last found for a major reconstruction and upgrading of the accommodation facilities that had now been in use for almost twenty years. The result of the improvements was top-class accommodation with the provision of three two-bedded rooms, three single rooms, a kitchen/dining room, a laboratory/lecture room, two bathrooms and a shower. The most important new facility for those working out of doors in Wester Ross's wet climate was a drying room. Naturally, its completion in April 1974 coincided with the Reserve's driest month on record of only 5.9 mm of rain.

The new hostel and laboratory facilities, attracting an increasing number of research workers, educational and voluntary groups, played a large part in Beinn Eighe's international nature conservation recognition and the award of the first of two International Designations. In 1976 the Reserve became a Biosphere Reserve under the UNESCO Man and the Biosphere programme, the aim of which is to 'conserve examples of characteristic ecosystems of the world's natural regions'. Beinn Eighe had earned this recognition and its place in the small and élite group of Biosphere Reserves in Britain.

In recounting the various routine events and developments that took place at Beinn Eighe over the twenty years up to the early 1970s, it is easy to forget the incredible impact that this most exciting of Reserves had on the succession of Wardens and Estate Workers who came and went over the years. Each brought with them a new zeal and a desire to see some kind of achievement in their time and it was the grandeur and remoteness of the area and the warmth of their reception that inspired them. Theaker, for example, who had come from the deep south, remembers driving up from Edinburgh with his wife and arriving in the dark of a November evening. They were ahead of their furniture so stayed in the hostel overnight and ate a meal prepared by Adeline, Dick Balharry's wife. All Wardens' wives over the years, and later the office administrators, have played an extremely important and often unrecorded role on the Reserve – often called out at awkward hours to help with tasks that were not in the job description. Of that night, Theaker remembers the sound of the rain and the roaring of the rutting stags.

For Campbell, whose first visit was as a volunteer, it was the breathtaking walk on the Mountain Trail that caught his imagination and brought him back every holiday for the next two years and finally onto the staff of the Nature Conservancy and, later, Scottish Natural Heritage at the Taynish Reserve in Argyllshire a few years later. Another future member of Scottish Natural Heritage, Ewen Cameron, also got his first taste of nature conservation management around that time. He served briefly as the Reserve's Summer Warden in 1977 and then went on to become Warden at Strathfarrar Reserve. Today he is the Area Officer for Deeside. Cameron came from a farming background on the Black Isle and the mountain of Beinn Eighe was his first experience of hill walking, a passion he has retained to this day.

Edwin and Mary-Anne Cross
in front of Anancaun.
Photo: R. Balharry

Theaker was followed as Warden in 1973 by Carmen Placido who describes his two years at Beinn Eighe as one of the happiest times of his life living in one of the most beautiful areas of the world. The following year Willie Lindsay took up the second permanent Estate Worker post, remaining at Beinn Eighe until 1992. As had several wives before and since, Ann Lindsay contributed much to the Reserve, including running the Visitor Centre for several years. Although there were times when there was little direct involvement by the Kinlochewe community in the Reserve, apart from contact with the few staff who lived in the village, nevertheless most of those who passed through Beinn Eighe – and in many senses *passed-out* from Beinn Eighe – have many memories and stories of involvement in village life. For example, many staff have been members of the Mountain Rescue Team or the Fire Service.

Their children too have been deeply affected, both by the place itself and by the feeling of belonging to such small and isolated communities, forging strong memories that have lasted throughout their lives. Edwin Cross was one of the very few staff at Beinn Eighe who actually came from the village of Kinlochewe and he and his wife, Mary-Anne, were very much part of the community where they still live today. Over the years Cross became an extremely experienced stalker and land manager, making a particular contribution to the care and welfare of the ponies. The next significant change in staffing occurred in 1977 when Ray Collier became Chief Warden for the North-West Region and we will come to the radical changes in management that occurred in his first ten years in the next chapter.

Crisis of direction in the woodland programme

Now we must return to the year 1973: the year of the Anancaun refurbishment and the Nature Conservancy's *annus horribilis* for both senior Scottish staff and Board members, and those working on National Nature Reserves whether as Wardens or research workers. It was the year that the Scottish Committee of the Conservancy was effectively demoted from one above all others, save the Great Britain Committee, to simply one among others. Its unique clout within the Conservancy disappeared. It was the year, too, that the Conservancy's research arm was torn off by Government and given an independent existence as the Institute of Terrestrial Ecology. Whereas the Conservancy's research staff had previously been intimately involved in nature conservation management on nature reserves, the new Nature Conservancy Council had, from then on, to contract this work from the Institute. The result was a sharp fall-off in research use of all Nature Reserves, including Beinn Eighe, and an immediate loss of rapport between research and conservation, to the detriment of both. On the positive side, the Conservancy became part of the Department of the Environment in 1973, rescued from the soup of the Natural Environment Research Council into which it had sunk from the public eye, almost without trace, in 1965, despite all the developments at Beinn Eighe.

However, it was other internal events in 1973, which were the catalysts for the last change in woodland restoration policy and caused widespread discussion of its future direction at all levels within the Conservancy for more than five years. Part of the reason for the prolonged discussions was the absence of a Management Plan from 1969, when the second revision reached its sell-by date, and the protracted preparations of a new Management Plan in the late 1970s. In fact, a new Management Plan did not emerge until 1990.

The year 1973 proved a poor one for pine seed production and, regardless of their previous promises of the supply of local provenance Scots pine, the Forestry Commission tree nursery could only offer to supply Beinn Eighe with 50,000 pine of Glen Affric origin. Despite the Conservancy's own stated requirement for seed of Wester Ross provenance these trees were accepted for the first of the last three enclosures and 34,000 were also accepted for the penultimate one in 1977. As had become the practice, both areas were ploughed, however the proportion of hardwoods, in the first at 30 per cent and the second at 48 per cent, was a great increase on previous plantings.

In the same year, Balharry, in his last year as Warden, initiated a wide and prolonged discussion with a paper entitled *A Case for Extensive Tree Planting.* He proposed that instead of continuing the fencing and planting of endless enclosures (ten to date) all remaining plantable ground below 236 m to the east and south of Coille na Glas Leitir, around 800 ha, should be planted up in one go, *without* fencing and following a reduction of 60 per cent of deer numbers. His thesis was that with a Reserve population of red deer of around fifty, that is a ratio of one deer to every 80 ha, enough trees would survive browsing and get away to create the woodland. Balharry's ratio is half the deer number that is generally accepted today as that which would allow successful natural regeneration. The reactions from senior staff were varied, but on the whole negative. There were many concerns: that such a reduction in deer numbers would have an adverse effect on the relative harmony of the Gairloch Conservation Unit; that the collection of enough suitable seed and the planting and fertilising of the tens of thousands of trees that would be required in such a short period would be a logistical nightmare; that at a cost of £50,000 it was far too expensive. Finally, that the result would be an even-age forest over a very large part of the Reserve. The clinching argument against the proposal was the risk factor: no one was prepared to make that level of investment without some guarantee of success and no one had tried such a scheme before.

Balharry had succeeded in accomplishing several radical changes at Beinn Eighe, but this was not going to be one of them. However, even though the proposal was turned down it *did* have the merit of re-igniting discussion on the basic principles of woodland restoration and was readdressed among several other proposals put forward by Niall Campbell in a draft paper in early 1978. This paper was intended to stimulate discussion, prior to a new Manament Plan planned for five years later and was almost an admission of failure: 'It is clear that many of the trees will never take on the appearance of "wild" Scots pine no matter how long they live – for instance already there are no lower limbs – and the mature trees will always resemble commercial timber.' Clearly Campbell viewed the widely spaced, multi-limbed trees of the relic pinewoods as the natural form of unmanaged Scottish native pinewoods. His deputy, Ball, rejected this view of the natural structure of the native pinewoods: 'There is a suggestion that we should try and create a copy of the existing pinewood remnants. This is a misconception because these forests are something of an unnatural freak,' and went on, a 'natural north western pinewood', would contain 'stands of tall, straight closely spaced trees of the same age class which have grown up together

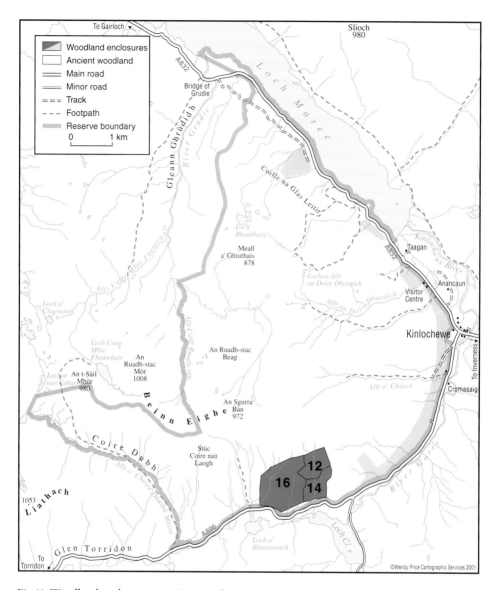

Fig 11 Woodland enclosures nos. 12, 14 and 16.

in the same clearing', as demonstrated in Norway's native forests and as hinted to by Pont in 1600. In response to Campbell's paper in the autumn of 1978, Boyd suggested there must be a plan for thinning, calling it: 'ecological thinning (which is a logical follow-up to the ecological planting which has been done all along).' In future, he suggested, we should continue using 'ecological forestry techniques', but he noted, careful planting can anticipate the problem thrown up by Campbell.

Summit heath
on the upper slopes
of Meall a' Ghiuthais.
Photo: SNH

The last small enclosures

The last three enclosures were situated on some of the poorest soils and in one of the most exposed tree-planting areas at the southern limit of the Reserve in Glen Torridon. Planting was to be between 200 m and 300 m, close to the upper limit of tree growth at Beinn Eighe. It was not surprising, therefore, that Scots pine growth was to be poorer here than in any of the plantings to date and that there was an almost complete failure of the hardwoods. Working conditions in this exposed area for the planters were not improved by the clothing provided at the time either. Michael Hughes, a volunteer for two winters, remembers struggling to plant trees on the hill in GPO-issue black PVC jacket, leggings, sou'wester and wellies of the day, designed for postmen crossing pavements in an occasional shower. Water seeped in around the neck and the top of the thighs above the leggings got soaked.

At almost the very same time as Boyd's reply to Campbell's paper in 1978, Collier, as Chief Warden, was in the act of ordering 40,000 Scots pines from the Forestry Commission nursery to plant in the final of the last three enclosures. The fencing materials for this had just been put out on the hill, but as yet no ploughing had been carried out. As a matter of routine, Collier informed both Ball and Peter Tilbrook (Deputy to Campbell from 1975 and latterly Regional Director) that the only Scots pine available and therefore ordered by him from the Commission, were once again of Glen Affric origin. By this point, however, their concerns over the distant origin of the seed had reached critical mass and they could not approve further planting of non-local provenance Scots pine. The matter therefore went to Campbell as Regional Officer.

Collier's argument was that approximately 90,000, pine of Glen Affric provenance had already been planted on the Reserve, mainly in the previous two enclosures over the last three years; that the fence was already going up, and that local provenance Scots pine would not be available until seed collected that year was ready for planting three years hence in 1981.

Others too, notably the Forestry Commission, had become concerned at the use of non-local provenance trees in planting programmes and by coincidence at this point, it introduced its new Native Pinewood Dedication Scheme which for the first time laid down rules requiring the use of local provenance native trees only. This event strengthened the arguments of Ball and Tilbrook against planting the Glen Affric pine. The position was now potentially embarrassing for the Conservancy. Here was the Government's 'ecological' body considering planting Scots pines on a National Nature Reserve that the Forestry Commission would not approve for planting on its own adjacent commercial plantations. Campbell agreed, therefore, that no more trees raised from Glen Affric seed should be planted, even though the last large enclosure was up and waiting. At this juncture there was no mention of the future of all the trees of Glen Affric origin already planted.

In May 1979 the many previous discussions, meetings, papers and proposals for future woodland regeneration culminated in yet another discussion paper. This time it was put forward by Tilbrook, as the first draft of the long-awaited new Management Plan. Tilbrook pointed out that there was no extant long-term objective for woodland expansion and that therefore it is assumed to be that: 'the long term aim is to expand the "natural type" of woodland to cover most (75 per cent) of the ground suitable for tree growth on the Reserve, i.e. the cover it is likely to have had but for man's influence', by which he meant that within this 75 per cent of suitable ground, planting could be preceded by ground preparation including ploughing where necessary. Tilbrook acknowledged that there was some disagreement within the Conservancy over the correctness of ploughing, planting and fertilising when the ultimate aim was to create a 'natural type' forest, and went on to say, '… it is maintained that such techniques are valid in the circumstances existing now at this Reserve'. In other words, ploughing and planting are now the established policy. He then reiterated the three options: continue with small enclosures over a long period; continue with larger enclosures over a shorter period; or employ saturation planting. Once again there were a variety of responses and opinions within the Conservancy, from supporting the second option as the least expensive and the best opportunity for creating a varied age structure, to returning to the original ideals of minimal intervention.

It seems that the more the woodland policy for Beinn Eighe was discussed and the more people became involved, the more confused it became: although it is true that very few staff now held to the original concept of expanding the native woodland from its core by natural regeneration only. One or two of the staff in Scotland at this time were openly critical of the rush to create woodland by ploughing, but no one appeared to be looking very far ahead. For example, there was a great deal of discussion on age classes and the need to ensure that an unnatural even-age class forest was not created. In hindsight we can see that age classes of up to five years' difference are hardly distinguishable after twenty or fifty years, never mind after a generation or two of conservationists. This can be seen today in an area planted between 1972 and 1974 on the Torridon Road, where variations in the planting habitat and perhaps planting quality, have resulted in a pinewood of a relatively even age but of very mixed structure. In a small area there are poor trees struggling in wet conditions among tall and healthy specimens three times their height. Anyway, as Ball had pointed out, mature native pinewood forests in Norway were of stands of even-aged, tall, straight trees. It must also have been the case that much of Coille na Glas Leitir itself would have been of even-age 250 years ago after the fire identified by McVean. However, the Conservancy, having by this point planted more than 300,000 Scots pine and 100,000 broadleaved trees, very shortly found that these points were perhaps the least of its concerns.

Regeneration and browsing

It is apparent that throughout the first thirty years of woodland management at Beinn Eighe, red deer were considered a hindrance to achieving the woodland goal and not a part of it. Although Beinn Eighe was considered to be unsuitable for the kind of classic behavioural studies undertaken at places such as Rum, with the construction of a number of enclosures, there arose opportunities for observing the effect of deer browsing on trees. Since at some stage it would no longer be practical, except with continual and considerable expense, to keep fences deer-proof, it was obviously necessary to determine at which stage in tree growth it would be safe to allow deer access.

In 1968 Balharry proposed that the top fence wires of one of the small diversification enclosures be taken down to allow access to deer. This proposal was agreed in principle and research began, in conjunction with Brian Mitchell and Brian Staines of the Institute of Terrestrial Ecology. The enclosure, planted on formerly agricultural ground, was at this stage a thicket of mainly ten-year-old, 3.6 m tall Scots pine. It was not considered worth the effort of monitoring the effects in any great detail and so, in 1969, after a photographic record was compiled, deer were allowed access. After one year deer had browsed the peripheral trees up to a height of about 2 m, had made little impression on the thicket, but had done considerable damage to the broadleaved trees.

The next enclosure to be used in this way was a very different proposition from the last, in that it was of 16 ha and situated within Coille na Glas Leitir with some natural regeneration. In 1970 this enclosure was divided in two by a fence and three tagged stags were put in each half from December 1971 to July 1972. When they were released they were found to be in poor condition. The main aim of this study was to see if red deer, by their browsing habit, would create structural diversity in a young plantation. Once again a photographic record was compiled and measurements of trees made along a transect. As with the previous experiment, dense pine was little affected, but broadleaved trees, particularly between 1.5 and 2 m in height *were* badly affected. It was considered that the deciduous trees would not grow beyond scrub if browsing were allowed to continue. This was taken to suggest that saturation planting without fencing would have been a very big risk, even though deer density in the enclosure was 1:3 ha, whereas Balharry had proposed a ratio of 1:80 ha. Similar grazing effect research was carried out later in 1979/80 at another enclosure by the same team and with similar results.

Despite some concern from the Scottish Director (Eggeling), in 1973 it was considered that trees were now sufficiently well grown to withstand deer browsing in a fourteen-year-old enclosure and so it was opened up to allow deer unrestricted access. Two years later girls from George Watson's College carried out a thorough survey. Their findings suggested that although there was severe damage to some trees, particularly to willow and rowan, the overall damage was acceptable and that therefore fourteen years was a suitable minimum age at which to open up enclosures to deer. The conclusions from these studies were written up by members of the Conservancy's Range Ecology Team and published in 1982.

Although this research was designed to illustrate the effect of deer on young trees, the effect of imposing a poor diet on the deer by their enclosure in a very limited area had, coincidentally, a profound influence on Balharry's ideas on selective culling of stags. Tradition had it that stags with poor heads should be killed as part of the annual population cull. The theory is that, if not, they pass on their poor antlers to the next generation. Their elimination therefore will eventually improve the head quality of the herd. At the time of its 'caging' within one of the enclosures, one of the captive stags, named Angus, was an eight pointer, that is having four points or tines on each antler. The following summer, after having been in the enclosure for seven months and having lost his antlers in the spring, he appeared as a 'switch', having only two single, poor antlers. One year later, having been contained once again within the better environment of the Anancaun fields, he not only lost his switch, but also blossomed into a ten-pointer – nurture more important than nature in this case.

Balharry's interest in deer management, personal commitment to the Gairloch Conservation Unit and belief that restoration of woodland should take place in the presence of red deer, meant that with his departure in the early 1970s, the attention to deer management became less focused and the annual cull level also fell. By the late 1970s both the overall cull levels and the individual cull number for each member of the Gairloch Conservation Unit, *including* those for Beinn Eighe, were set at a recommended one-sixth level of the population. This level of cull, however, is designed to keep the deer population stable and not necessarily to allow natural regeneration of native woodland. There was a gentleman's agreement at this time between the Conservancy and one of its neighbours, whereby the latter would take most of the stags and Beinn Eighe would cull more hinds, the arrangement, however, was not successful. Effectively the Conservancy lost some of its influence on deer numbers in the area, even on its own ground. The level of incursion of deer into the enclosures at that time is illustrated in May 1979, when fourteen stags, one hind and her calf were found within one of the restoration enclosures. It was to be another eight years before the issue of deer management was readdressed.

Calgary mares and foal
on the hill.
Photo: R. Balharry

8 Back to basics 1980–91

'Minimal intervention and the precautionary principle again became the key management principles …'

T. Clifford & A. N. Forster, 1997

Planting hits the buffers

The year 1980 heralded the last major change to woodland restoration policy over Beinn Eighe's first fifty years. In that year G I Forrest, of the Forestry Commission Research Station at Roslin, produced a seminal paper on regional variation in the biochemistry of Scots pine across Scotland. Although the science has perhaps not stood the test of time, the most important of its findings, as far as Beinn Eighe is concerned, appear to be supported by further research in the 1980s and 1990s. The paper was to have serious implications for the selection of seed for restoration of native pine forests and for commercial planting in Scotland: it was entitled *Genotypic Variation among Native Scots Pine Populations in Scotland based on Monoterpene Analysis* (1980).

Monoterpenes are biochemicals that occur in a wide range of plants and that had earlier been the subject of several studies of Scots pine across Europe and Russia. Forrest sampled the monoterpenes of Scots pine right across native pine forests in Scotland and identified six distinctive groupings. Research into mitochondrial DNA of Scots pine in the 1990s did not support the existence of these six groupings, but it did confirm Forrest's findings that by far the most distinctive pines in Scotland were those of Wester Ross: Shieldaig, West Coulin (Loch Clair), Loch Maree, Coille na Glas Leitir and the Loch Maree islands. The division lies between the West Coulin pines by Loch Clair, just across the road from the Beinn Eighe Reserve, and the East Coulin pines only 2.5 km distant at Easan Dorcha, above Glen Carron. This seems an incredibly short distance between two races of trees; it is not even across a watershed, although there is a hill between the pinewoods. One can only assume that the prevailing winds have always been westerly or southwesterly and that only insignificant amounts of pollen have ever made their way from East Coulin, north and west to West Coulin. But the story does not end there.

The principal deviation that made the Wester Ross group so different from all the other Scottish pinewoods lay in its low values for one particular monoterpene. Significantly, in Europe this low value is a characteristic of Scots pine of southern areas, such as south France, Spain, north Italy. 'Conceivably …' Forrest suggests, this Wester Ross group, 'could represent the relics of the first invasion northwards from Spain and France, while other areas to the south and east could have been colonised at a later stage from more northerly Continental areas after the ice-sheets had receded northward and disappeared from eastern Scotland.' The hypothesis that 8500 years ago Scots pine replaced birch and hazel woodlands earlier in the North-West than in the Central and Eastern Highlands of Scotland is supported by other research into the pollen content of peat in the area.

Forrest suggests that with the ice melting more quickly on the west coast of Scotland, under the influence of milder Atlantic weather, a tongue of Scots pine, the only relics of which are now in Wester Ross, crept up from Ireland and farther south, and established itself around the Beinn Eighe area. As the climate improved, pine established farther south was replaced by broadleaved woodland. Thus when the later invasion of pine from Europe moved westward, as the main mass of ice on the Scottish mountains melted, it met up with its southern cousins at Coulin and perhaps elsewhere. Another, less likely hypothesis, is that the Wester Ross pine might have originated from pine that survived the Ice Age, but on land that has since submerged under the rising sea following the melting of the ice sheet.

Some of the very first Conservancy staff to visit Beinn Eighe in the early 1950s commented on the different form of the Wester Ross pine trees when compared with those of the Central Highlands of Scotland. Steven & Carlisle, in *The Native Pinewoods of Scotland* (1959), inferred that these trees must be particularly adapted to the relatively wet climate. It has also been known for some time that pine trees from Wester Ross grow less well in Central Scotland and vice versa. These physical differences therefore, may reflect a genetic difference. The implications for the woodland restoration project on Beinn Eighe, of a unique genotype of native pine in Wester Ross, were very serious. If these trees are significantly different then this is a unique gene pool of pine adapted over thousands of years to a relatively wet climate, not just on the fringes of the Scottish pinewoods, but on the oceanic fringes of the great European pine forests: the extreme western limit of their world distribution. There are also implications for other species characteristic of the Wester Ross pinewoods, some of which are being followed up. For example, juniper at Beinn Eighe has been found to be different from other junipers in Scotland. Could it too have been an earlier coloniser and are there others?

The findings were thought to be of such significance that the Forestry Commission, following the introduction of its Native Pinewood Dedication Scheme a year or two earlier, recommended that in order to preserve the genetic integrity of the different pine groups, there should be no transference of seeds or plants across groups. One of the first results of this Forestry Commission policy was that it would not recognise the West Coulin Scots pine as a native seed source for the Wester Ross group, unless the adjacent Scots pine of Glen Affric provenance were removed from the Reserve. This once again raised the issue of the provenance of tens of thousands of Glen Affric pine already planted. But this time a decision on their future would have to be taken.

Coincidentally, when Campbell's decision to halt the planting of non-local provenance pine had already been taken, in 1980, the Forestry Commission tree nursery on the Black Isle closed, cutting off the supply of all the Glen Affric pine seedlings that had been used latterly on the Reserve and that had been planned for use in the very last enclosure. This event and the implications of the monoterpene research therefore added further weight to the arguments of Ball, Tilbrook and others who were pressing for the planting of local pine only. The planting programme in the early 1980s was therefore confined to a relatively small number of broadleaves: alder, rowan and birch with some spot sowings of oak.

The Conservancy then took the first tentative steps in the removal of Glen Affric trees from enclosures opposite to West Coulin. In the same year, Sandy MacLennan of the Conservancy's Inverness office produced an internal discussion paper on the Wester Ross provenance, supported by maps. These delineated strict seed source zonations for all the native pine groups *within* the main Wester Ross group recognised by Forrest. These zonations were subsequently refined by Tim Clifford (who became the Beinn Eighe Warden in 1984) and by Iain MacGowan in 1989, who drew up boundaries following the watersheds, which act as natural barriers to pollen flow and seed movement. On Beinn Eighe, this identified three areas and laid down that the seed for any future planting within one area should preferably only come from that area. In retrospect this appears to have been a very narrow and severe interpretation of the limits of seed or pollen dispersal, but at the time the Conservancy was determined to follow the precautionary principle and act on the best information available. It also has to be viewed as a reaction to what had become a rather casual attitude to the methods of achieving the aims of woodland restoration.

New Wardens, new visions

Clifford had arrived in 1984 to take over one of the Warden posts following the departure of Hugh Brown, with the other post still being held by Cross. He had been working as a Warden on a National Nature Reserve in Lincolnshire and had been intrigued by the Reserve ever since he had camped there one summer as a student. He brought a new enthusiasm to and, perhaps for the first time, a scientific bent to the role of Warden at Beinn Eighe. Welcomed as he and his wife Alice were to the Reserve, it was nothing to the welcome their five children received from the Kinlochewe schoolteacher, Margaret McLean, for the school was near to closing due to the lack of pupils and the Clifford family ensured its immediate future. By that year, Brown and Cross had overseen nine years of steady progress in the woodland restoration programme with the planting of around 150,000 trees. The annual deer cull had continued at one-sixth of the population, the captive deer continued to attract a few visitors into Anancaun and the New Calgary stud bequeathed by Mrs Warren continued to be bred and cared for to ensure the stud's survival.

The late 1970s and early 1980s however, were years of change, both at Beinn Eighe and elsewhere in the Conservancy. Balharry moved on as Chief Warden for the North-West Region and was replaced by Collier in 1977. On the wider front the Conservancy published its mammoth and comprehensive Nature Conservation Review (of Britain) that year, compiled by the Chief Scientist, Derek Ratcliffe. By this time, after twenty-six years, the Conservancy had established 153 National Nature Reserves covering around 120,465 ha. Conservationists and others might have had reason to believe then that surely the most important areas of Britain for natural and geological conservation, such as Beinn Eighe, must now be under protection. Not a bit of it, the Review identified a staggering 735 sites, covering almost one million ha of National Nature Reserve status. Only one-tenth of the job had therefore been accomplished. However, there were other events in the Conservancy's programme that would keep its attention focused elsewhere.

With the passing of the Wildlife and Countryside Act (1981) heralding a broader role for the Conservancy in the wider countryside and with a Government directive that the Conservancy must re-notify all of the 1000 or so Sites of Special Scientific Interest within a short timetable, there followed an abrupt change in the Conservancy's priorities. Many new Area and specialist staff were taken on to cope with this pressure and there was naturally a concomitant reduction in funds for National Nature Reserve management, right across Britain. This was the era of the Scottish Conservancy's unsought confrontations with landowners and forestry over compensation on a number of Sites of Special Scientific Interest – a time when Reserves were pushed well to the back of the public mind. In 1984, the ultimate responsibility for overseeing the implementation of these changes in the North-West, and Beinn Eighe in particular, fell to Tilbrook, who became Regional Officer in that year. Clifford's arrival therefore coincided with a time of change and possible staff and financial restrictions.

However, the award of the Reserve's second international designation, the European Diploma, by the Committee of Ministers of the Council of Europe in 1983, had a major beneficial impact on future financial allocations to Beinn Eighe. This award was a great honour, recognising both the importance of the wildlife of Beinn Eighe and the outstanding quality of management in its protection and enhancement. Beinn Eighe was the first of only five British sites so far to gain this award.

The Diploma is awarded for periods of five years and lays down conditions that the site must fulfil before its quinquennial reassessment and renewal. Tilbrook made the presentation on behalf of Beinn Eighe at Strasburg and scientific advisers to the Council of Europe visited Beinn Eighe to make an assessment of the situation and suggest conditions, prior to the Council's final decision. To an extent, of course, these conditions were those that the Beinn Eighe management team ideally wished to see carried out and themselves brought to the attention of the Council. Although no financial grant comes with the award, it pressures national governments to fulfil whatever conditions have been laid down: it would be a political embarrassment if an award was withdrawn due to lack of fulfilment of the conditions. In the case of Beinn Eighe, the Council's conditions included several that swung the woodland management policy back towards first principles from which it had deviated over the years. The first for example stated: '… the planting of indigenous species … must be carried out using the local genetic stock and in accordance with ecological principles [i.e., plant several small areas each year].' In other words: no more ploughing and no more wall-to-wall Scots pine.

Another condition related to the removal of the exotic trees in the Forestry Commission enclosure erected in 1959 which were to have been removed once the native trees they were sheltering had grown. This was taken up almost immediately and negotiations between the Conservancy and Commission for the former's resumption of the lease began in 1984. It was to take five years to complete negotiations, during which there were regular misunderstandings between the bureaucrats of both organisations. At one point in 1987, the Commission published a list of locations, including its enclosure at Beinn Eighe, that it was considering *selling*. This raised temperatures considerably. In 1989 the resumption was finally completed and the Conservancy could begin to plan the removal of exotic conifers and non-local provenance Scots pine from within it.

On becoming Regional Officer (later Regional Director) for the North West, Tilbrook was keen to see the result of thirty years of recorded research and management put to some use. He therefore called in the Conservancy's Field Survey Unit to investigate the records. Clifford remembers a summer searching Coille na Glas Leitir with a colleague from Edinburgh for McVean's experimental plots from the early 1950s: alas, most could not be found. The lesson, however, was learned and long-term transects for monitoring, in addition to fixed-point photographs, were established for the future.

This collaboration between the Region and the Headquarters scientific staff, which coincided with the need to know the provenance of all Scots pine planting to date, resulted in student assistance being employed to search the records of thirty years of planting on the Reserve. From this it gradually became clear that in several cases there had been mixed-provenance plantings and it was not always clear on the ground which was which. The approach to the removal of all non-local provenance pines, therefore, had to be a pragmatic one, accepting the implications that their removal would take many years, divert energy and resources from expanding the restoration programme and, inevitably, cast a shadow of doubt over many years of work on the Reserve. Undoubtedly, some mistakes were probably made in the identification of non-local provenance planting and local provenance trees have been unnecessarily removed, but the result had to err on the precautionary side.

The preceding pages describe the enormous problems that were created for those responsible for Beinn Eighe by the discovery of the uniqueness of the Wester Ross Scots pine and no doubt staff were not looking forward to having to negate many years of work by the removal of the Glen Affric provenance trees. On the other hand, the discovery was a revelation and a substantial justification for the protection and restoration of Coille na Glas Leitir. The whole issue of these non-local trees was addressed in the preparation of the third Management Plan, 1990–4, prepared by Clifford. The production of the Plan, however, was preceded by several radical changes in management, three of which were designed to make savings in time and money and could only have been viewed rather negatively by the Reserve staff at the time.

Captive deer and ponies out, nursery in

The minutes of the Reserve Management Group of 13 March 1986 record an agreement among members that, as soon as possible: 'The captive red deer herd to be disposed of; Pony stud … to be sold; Tree nursery to be re-established; Inbye land [at Anancaun] to be rented out for grazing or into croft land; Priority to be given to refurbishing Anancaun Field Station.'

The deer in the paddock by Anancaun, on the low ground outwith the Reserve, were the last of the captive animals accumulated by Balharry. By now the Nature Trails and the Visitor Centre at Aultroy were available for visitors and they were no longer being encouraged to visit Anancaun, now an office as well as home for some of the staff. The removal of the deer to a farm in Fife relieved the Reserve staff from winter-feeding and maintenance of deer paddock fences. This was a fairly straightforward operation and although the staff missed their presence, the loss was not so hard to take as that of the ponies in 1987, to which they and the local community had naturally become attached over the sixteen years since they had been bequeathed by Mrs Warren.

The terms of the endowment that came with the ponies required them to be maintained as a stud and their progeny registered with the Highland Pony Society. The mares were therefore regularly put to the stallion and the best of the fillies retained as the original mares grew past their working life. By the mid-1980s, however, following the erection of the enclosures, most stalking was on the lower steep ground within Coille na Glas Leitir. This is quite unsuitable terrain for ponies and quite close to the road so the ponies were being used less and less, apart from occasionally being hired out to adjacent Estates. Like the captive deer, they required winter-feeding, the fields required management and the foals required training and care. Reserve staff carried out those tasks, but in the 1970s especially, the last was regularly taken over by a volunteer, Betsy Giles.

Betsy Giles had spent 1969 with Mrs Warren and the New Calgary Stud in Sussex, prior to the latter's death and the ponies' move to Beinn Eighe. Subsequently, she herself bought two of the New Calgary ponies before she arrived at Beinn Eighe in 1970 to see if she could be of assistance. This was welcomed and for the rest of the 1970s and into the 1980s she regularly visited

Beinn Eighe to handle and train the foals. Her contribution undoubtedly relieved the Reserve staff of much work, but it also ensured that the surplus foals were trained before being sold and therefore fetched better prices. In 1978 she married Conservancy Stalker Lewis McRae and thereafter occasionally also helped with the Rum ponies when her husband made his annual visits to that Reserve for its deer cull.

Because of the nature of Mrs Warren's endowment, the Conservancy were required to take great care in the disposal of the ponies. It was essential to ensure that they would go to a good home and be retained there as a pedigree stud. The word of their sale quickly spread among the cognoscenti and before the sale notice had even been published, interest had been expressed by a number of potential buyers. Word spread as far as France where the Ligue Français pour la Protection des Oiseaux was looking for ponies to graze coastal grassland at their Reserve des Marais d'Yves near La Rochelle. Grazing management there was required to ensure the conservation of grassland habitat for meadow birds, such as the skylark. Coincidentally, the Ligue already had twenty-one Scottish Blackface sheep grazing on Ré Island Reserve nearby.

Since Mrs Warren had originally planned for her ponies to live on a Scottish National Nature Reserve, it seemed very appropriate to renew the 'auld alliance' and send the ponies to a French Reserve rather than dispose of them in a private sale. There is even a Highland Pony Society in France with whom the Ligue promised to consult and, as it guaranteed to keep to the terms of Mrs Warren's bequest, the ponies were gifted to it in 1987. Fittingly, Cross, who had looked after them for seventeen years, also made the journey to France, to ensure the ponies would be properly cared for in their new home. The following year, after twenty years of service at Beinn Eighe, longer than anyone before or since, Cross left for Creag Meagaidh National Nature Reserve.

Following the departure of the deer and ponies, plans were then put in hand to dispose of much of the inbye land at Anancaun, excepting, of course, the area required for re-establishing the nursery which had been closed for sixteen years. The decision to reopen the nursery was taken to ensure complete confidence in the exact source of seed for all future planting, as it had been found that this could not be guaranteed even when using a very reputable private nursery. This was not a decision taken lightly, for running a tree nursery is a major, year-round commitment.

At that time it required several seed beds and a large area for transplant lines. Once seedlings had been transferred to transplant lines, following one or two year's growth, the previous year's saplings had to be uplifted for planting on the hill. Then the seedbeds had to be re-sown, usually with a rotation of oats and tares to restore good soil conditions. On top of that, both seedbeds and transplant lines had to be weeded and irrigated throughout the summer, often in the most trying wet or midge-plagued conditions.

Pine seedlings
in the Anancaun tree nursery
two years after re-opening in 1987.
Photo: SNH

Because of the substantial time commitment of staff and volunteers to this traditional mode of nursery management, the Conservancy began to look around for new and less time-consuming techniques. These were introduced in the early 1990s, initially under the care of Lindsay who had now been fourteen years on the Reserve, and the other Estate Worker, Eoghain Maclean. The native tree nursery was Lindsay's special forte and he went on to develop one in his own garden when he retired. Maclean had come to live in the Kinlochewe area at the age of six, and started as an Estate Worker in 1986. He is still at Beinn Eighe today, now as the Deputy Reserve Manager. Three years after its reopening in 1987 the new nursery produced its first trees. Two years later planting resumed after a gap of five years.

Fulfilling diploma conditions

A third refurbishment of the Field Station became a priority for management in 1986 as it was a condition of the 1983 European Diploma award that: '… as a matter of urgency, the funds needed for Anancaun Field Station to become fully operational should be made available as soon as possible, so that it can support all the major projects listed in the management plan (egg. surveys, surveillance, research, development).'

The Field Station and related buildings at Anancaun had last been refurbished in 1973 and maintained only at a minimal level since, due to the general squeeze on funds within the Conservancy. With the backing of the European Diploma the work, costing £65,000, was completed in April 1988, supervised by Tom Cane, the Region's Buildings Officer. Lord James Douglas-Hamilton, Scottish Office Minister for Home Affairs, officially opened the new Field Centre that now consisted of a lounge/lecture room, laboratory, kitchen, dining room and four bed/bunk rooms with space for fourteen. The benefits that the new facilities brought to the management and educational use of Beinn Eighe were amply demonstrated in 1988 when around twenty educational, research and voluntary groups made use of the accommodation and research facilities. These included students from Oxford, Edinburgh, Aberdeen and Norway, as well as three visits from the Scottish Conservation Projects Trust, including one from their Upland Footpath Team who worked on the Mountain Trail. A by-product of the new

Norwegian students
surveying
in Coille na Glas Leitir
in 1988.
Photo: T. Clifford

Field Station was the addition of a few more shoppers to Kinlochewe, although the large visiting groups tended to bring in their own food.

The purpose of the visits of most of these groups was educational, but several came for research purposes. For example, the students from Norway were involved in a joint project with the Conservancy to try and establish the reason for long-term changes to the health and shape of the crowns of Scots pine. Other projects that occurred that year included one on the level and possible threat of acid rain and a second on the establishment of a system for the recording of long-term changes in the ancient semi-natural woodland. There were also more than ten biological surveys covering groups that ranged from moths and dragonflies to pine marten, and from rare plants to upland lochs and lochans. Not content with that level of occupancy at the Field Centre, Clifford and Bill Taylor, who had joined the Reserve as the Warden replacement for Cross, made plans to target universities and colleges to increase the level of its use. Research and survey needs of the Reserve were also drawn up so that potential students could be targeted. In

Anancaun in 1983,
prior to third refurbish-
ment.
Photo: SNH

the following year there was a marked increase in use of the Field Centre from 900 to 1985 bed-nights, of which more than a third were long-term volunteers, a little less than a third were Scottish Conservation Projects who worked on the trails and in the nursery, and another third research and survey students. By 1991 the figure for bed-nights had increased to 2255, of which nearly half were long-term volunteers.

Prior to Beinn Eighe, Taylor had been a Ranger in a Country Park. When he arrived in 1988, the interpretive materials in the Visitor Centre had not been changed for over a decade. Interpretation just happened to be Taylor's particular strength and over the winter 1988/9 he restructured and upgraded the interpretive material. He and Clifford also moved out of the tin shack that had served as the Reserve office up to that point and he recalls an anecdote that illustrates the office conditions of the time. He had changed the ribbon of the typewriter just before Christmas and when he returned to the shed to use it after the holiday, he noticed that the ribbon had completely disappeared inside the typewriter. On opening it up he found the ribbon wound into a neat little mouse nest under the keys.

Visitors to the Centre were of the order of 6000 in the mid 1980s. By 1988 they had risen to 7232 and by 1990 to just over 10,000. It was estimated that this probably only represented about a quarter of the total number of visitors to the Reserve. As part of the requirement of the European Diploma award in 1983, preliminary visitor surveys, by both Aberdeen and Edinburgh University students, were carried out to establish the main features of visitor interest. The results showed that the Woodland and Mountain Trails were particularly attractive and that these facilities were drawing people into the area and bringing financial benefits to the local communities.

In 1984, the Mountain Trail was closed for safety reasons. After three years of intensive work by the Scottish Conservation Corps, staff and volunteers it was reopened by the local MP Charles Kennedy to mark the European Year of the Environment in 1987. The opening was part of a very successful Open Day for visitors. Bill McKenzie, a senior administrator at the Edinburgh Headquarters, wrote to North-West staff after the event to congratulate them on yet another national and international first at Beinn Eighe: '… the first buffet lunch associated with a National Nature Reserve event to include home made clootie dumpling'.

In 1988, when the European Diploma was due for its quinquennial reappraisal, part of the inbye at Anancaun was exchanged with an adjacent landowner for a strip of ancient woodland contiguous with the Reserve, fulfilling the last of the 1983 Diploma conditions within the five years and it was therefore renewed for a further five years. There is no doubt that the 1980s saw one of the great pulses of achievement on the Reserve, entirely due to the drive of the Reserve staff with the support of the Region. A similar period of innovation and advance as occurred during the initial years under McVean and later years under Balharry and Boyd.

Monitoring regeneration
in deep heather
along fixed transect.
Photo: D. Miller

Bryophytes and hoverflies

As the 1980s progressed, the amount of research
and survey carried out on the Reserve, particularly
of many of the lesser known groups and species,
steadily increased. Clifford and Taylor carried out
some of this work themselves, such as the survey
of rare and montane plants that had not been
monitored for a number of years and the setting
up of monitoring transects to gauge the rate of
natural regeneration within the woodland. A
baseline survey of bryophytes, one of the
outstanding features of the Reserve, and base line
surveys of lichens, were undertaken in 1988. In
1989 research work was carried out on distribution
of prostrate juniper on the plateau, Scots pine
pollen accumulation on bog and moss surfaces,
and the ecology of the Atlantic mosses and
liverworts, among several others. The following
year research was carried out on the ecology of the mountain heath and the effects
on it of deer trampling, and the distribution and ecology of the very rare leafy
liverwort *Herbertus borealis* that grows within it. In 1991 there were no less than
four Honours theses completed on Beinn Eighe. Several of these pieces of survey
and research, including those in the 1990s, confirmed the national and
international importance of the flora and fauna of Beinn Eighe.

One of the most interesting pieces of research and conservation carried out at
this time focused on the little-studied insects of the Reserve. Iain MacGowan, an
entomologist in his spare time, was an Area Officer covering the area of Beinn
Eighe in the late 1980s and had carried out surveys of pinewood insects across
Scotland. Very unexpectedly he found a few larvae of the hoverfly *Callicera rufa*
at Beinn Eighe, which in Britain is confined to the remnants of the Caledonian
pine forest. This hoverfly is one of those rare species, categorised in the bible of
rare species – the *Red Data* book – as 'in danger of extinction and whose survival
is unlikely unless management is implemented'. It is also recognised by the
Council of Europe as an indicator species for 'forests of international importance
to nature conservation'.

The larvae of this species develop in water-filled rot holes in the crook between
the trunk and the branches of pines. In the west of Scotland, for one reason or
another, pines lack rot holes. In the whole of Coille na Glas Leitir, MacGowan
found only two good rot holes, though both contained the larvae of the hoverfly.
The population at Beinn Eighe was clearly at a very low ebb. As an act of active
conservation research MacGowan cut an artificial rot hole in a tree within 300 m

of the largest natural rot hole with larvae. The following year he returned to find it occupied by the hoverfly. He then went on to make three more rot holes, all of which became occupied within three years. By those simple acts of management the population of this rare insect at Beinn Eighe has probably been secured. Further work on the invertebrates by MacGowan showed that there were far fewer pine wood specialists at Beinn Eighe than in the drier pine woods to the east, further demonstrating the unique nature of these woodlands at the extreme western edge of their range.

The ring fence

The renewal of the European Diploma in 1988 meant that Beinn Eighe was now getting a greater proportion of the North-West Region's funding than it had been given for a number of years. As a result of the removal of the deer and ponies more attention could now be focused on the woodland programme, interpretation for visitors and encouragement of the use of the Field Station. The Diploma also provided the impetus for securing the second seasonal Estate Worker as a permanent post, bringing the staffing level of the Reserve up to four full-time posts. It also added weight to a proposal that had been in the air when the first enclosures were being discussed: would it not be cheaper and more efficient in the long run to erect one large enclosure rather than a whole lot of small ones? The position had been reached when virtually all the ground by the roadside had been fenced and planted, from the south-eastern fringes of Coille na Glas Leitir, right around almost to the boundary with The National Trust for Scotland in Glen Torridon, so the time was right.

With the support of Tilbrook it was proposed that a very ambitious Ring Fence of 7 km should be erected to link the far ends of these enclosures across the shoulder of Beinn Eighe to enclose an area of some 1100 ha, within which it was planned to take forward the new woodland management proposals. To an extent,

The completed Ring Fence snakes away around the flanks of Beinn Eighe.
Photo: SNH

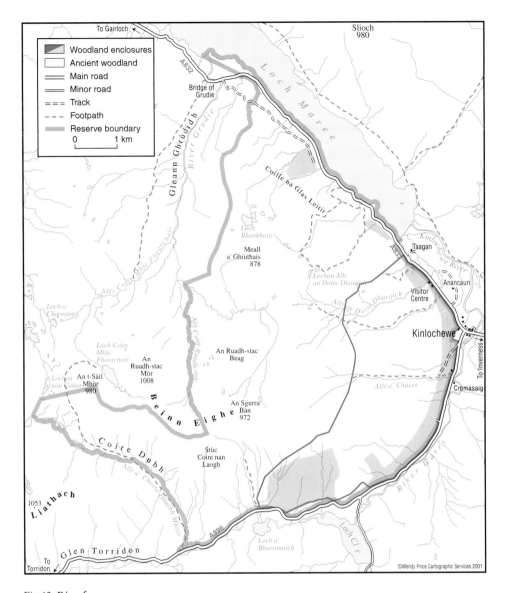

Fig 12 **Ring fence.**

the erection of this fence was a reflection of the inability of the Conservancy to influence neighbouring estates to reduce their deer populations to a level that would allow natural regeneration. There was considerable discussion on the principle of the Ring Fence within the Conservancy and with the neighbouring estates, some of which were strongly opposed to a substantial reduction in the deer range, particularly of wintering ground. It has to be remembered that this was a very large-scale enclosure in the 1980s, although today there are quite a number of private schemes of this order in the North-West Highlands.

The planning of the fence was both a swansong for Cross and a baptism for Maclean. In 1986, the latter spent almost two months marking out the best line across the hill to ensure the minimum damage to the fence from snow and the best ground for fence poles, although in many places stanchions had to be set into bare rock. Maclean recalls returning to Anancaun after a day surveying, high and remote on the hill, and describing to Cross a piece of ground and the dilemma he faced in choosing a fence line. From years of stalking, Cross knew the exact piece of ground Maclean described and was able to advise him on the best fence line to avoid snowdrifts.

Two years later in 1988, after Cross's departure, the fence was completed, enclosing all the ground below 370 m, a little above the tree line and all the earlier enclosures, barring one in Coille na Glas Leitir and another protecting the high-level tall-herb community. The former was removed in the early 1990s leaving the woodland open to deer grazing, while the latter is still maintained. While the Ring Fence was being completed the Reserve Estate staff of Lindsay and Maclean, set about upgrading the 4 km of ageing fencing along the Torridon roadside with the help of volunteers. Starting in November 1988, they somehow managed to replace 1 km by Christmas and the remainder in the following year. Before the final closure of the fence, deer that had broken into the Forestry Commission enclosure through the old fence were driven out with help from the Kinlochewe community. At the same time, to compensate for the loss of ground to red deer and to further reduce the grazing pressure in Coille na Glas Leitir, the Reserve cull was increased substantially. Within the Ring Fence forty-four stags were culled and a further eighteen stags and fifteen hinds outwith. The following year the first planting of trees took place within the fence. Planting policy this time was to be very different to that which had predominated for the last decade.

Go back to go

There had been no new Management Plan for the Reserve for almost twenty years, it is unsurprising therefore that staff took the opportunity to set out definitively, for the first time, a rationale and detailed programme to meet the principal aims of the Reserve that had been so passionately debated in the early 1950s.

In contrast to its predecessors, the 1990–4 Management Plan for Beinn Eighe was a very thorough document: the fact that it set out twenty-seven Operational Objectives is a reflection of its thoroughness. The key points as far as woodland restoration is concerned were: 'the re-creation of *natural-type* pine/birch forest of varied pattern and structure on deforested areas of the Reserve below the present climatic tree line'; maintenance of 'the broad genetic integrity of the Reserve's native Scots pine woodland'; and eradication of 'exotic conifers and shrubs'.

The Primary Objective prescribed the 'naturalness' of future woodland management: 'The management of the existing ancient woodland, in the presence of native deer, to maximise natural processes (nutrient cycling, natural regeneration, competition, predation and self-thinning).' Other objectives relating to the woodland were: to 'create a diversity of woodland habitats', and the areas above the wood; to 'extend the area of … sub-alpine type scrub and develop a natural transition between this … and the main woodland'; and 'where soils and drainage will allow, the eventual establishment of a woodland ecosystem', a qualification that replaced the formerly accepted principle that planting could take place where soils and drainage could be modified by ploughing. The new attitudes were summed up in a later paper by Clifford and Forster in *Scottish Woodland History* (1997) as: '… a move away from any attempt to re-create some idealised concept of pine-dominated woodland at the post-glacial climatic optimum, towards the restoration of woodland processes as they would function under the climatic and edaphic regimes prevalent today.'

The primary aim within the Ring Fence enclosure was therefore to take forward these ideas by allowing the natural expansion of the three ravine relicts of native woodland – Allt an Doire Dharaich, Allt à Chùirn and Allt Sguabaig – while only planting natural groupings of trees on suitable soils in areas distant from these ravines. In a return to the original 'ecological' principles, a vegetation survey was carried out before any planting occurred. Previously, vegetation surveys to guide planting had been carried out by staff such as McVean and Wallace. By the late 1980s however, the Conservancy had developed the National Vegetation Classification, a sophisticated system that identified every vegetation community in the country from its key components and placed it in a matrix, allowing national comparisons. On Beinn Eighe, the Classification was used to identify both 'open ground' vegetation communities on which trees should not be planted and suitable vegetation types that would support a variety of woodland communities. It revealed that only about 20 per cent, or 240 ha, of scattered patches within the ring-fenced area, were suitable for planting. A description of the latter communities was then simplified for the planters, usually conservation volunteers, to ensure that the various species of trees were planted in the correct vegetation type. Ground preparation also reverted to the simplest and least intrusive method. Using only a spade, vegetation was cleared, a notch made or a turf cut out and inverted or a small mound of soil raised, and each seedling was given a handful of fertiliser. Thus began the 1990s.

The new NNR threshold sign.
Photo: D. Miller

9 Responsibilities and commitments widen 1992–2001

'Tha 'n eilide anns an fhrìth
Mar bu chòir dhi bhith
Far am faigh i mìlteach
Glan-feòirneanach;'

'The hind is in the forest
as she ought to be,
where she may have sweet grass,
clean, fine bladed;'

Donnchadh Mac an t-Saoir,
'Moladh Beinn Dobhrain'

Duncan Ban MacIntyre,
'Praise of Ben Dobhrain'

A new organisation

In terms of funding and staff, the early and middle years of the last decade of the century were perhaps some of the most challenging for the Beinn Eighe Reserve since its establishment. In 1990, under the Environmental Protection Act (1990), the Nature Conservancy Council of Great Britain was split into three parts. The following year, under the Natural Heritage (Scotland) Act (1991), the Nature Conservancy Council Scotland amalgamated with the Countryside Commission for Scotland to become Scottish Natural Heritage. Meanwhile, the English branch of the Conservancy became English Nature; the Welsh branch, also amalgamating with its Countryside Commission, became the Countryside Council for Wales; and across the Irish Sea, the Environment and Heritage Service (Northern Ireland) was formed.

For Scotland (and Wales), where the new Government body had to integrate the staff and combine the aims of the two previous organisations, this was a time of great change and uncertainty. In effect, the twin countryside roles, split by the Government committees of the late 1940s into National Parks and Nature Reserves, were reunited in Scotland and Wales. The new Scottish Natural Heritage became responsible not only for the safeguard of wildlife on statutory sites, such as National Nature Reserves, and the provision of advice on nature conservation, but also responsible for landscape, access and recreation, and support to Country Parks and their Ranger services. At the same time the term 'natural environment' became replaced by the term 'natural heritage', reflecting the new organisation's wider remit.

Right from the beginning of the Nature Conservancy there was an internal division between the 'scientists' and the 'field' or Warden staff. Scottish Natural Heritage removed that division at a stroke, abolishing the post of Warden, integrating all staff and giving them broader roles and responsibilities. Only on a few of the largest Reserves in Scotland, including two owned by Scottish Natural Heritage, Rum and Beinn Eighe, were on-site management posts – Reserve Managers – retained. The resources of Scottish Natural Heritage were put under great strain in those early years of the new organisation. Reserve management had taken a large proportion of the total budget in the old Nature Conservancy Council, but now those funds were seen to be needed elsewhere, at least for the moment. The redirected input of the new organisation to the wider countryside and into Country Parks had immediate benefits for the natural heritage and for the people of Scotland, but there was a reduction in resources for Reserves. At Beinn Eighe itself, it was planned to integrate Area staff (those with a wider remit in the Wester Ross area) with those on the Reserve by making use of the existing buildings. In the longer term this has been proved to be far-sighted, in that the Reserve staff are no longer relatively isolated from wider experience and developments, while the Area staff are equally aware of the management experience and demonstration potential on their doorstep. At that time, however, the office accommodation at Anancaun was not yet ready and some of the staff had to share temporary accommodation in a portacabin, which did not make ideal working conditions.

In practical terms, the Reserve Manager, Clifford, found himself giving 20 per cent of his time to new responsibilities outwith the Reserve, and he wrote: 'With the general lack of commitment towards NNR management at present and the gloomy outlook for staffing at Beinn Eighe I am becoming increasingly concerned about our abilities to fulfil the management objectives …'

The formation of Scottish Natural Heritage also saw the introduction of a new breed of professional staff into the organisation who ran a tight ship. Perhaps this was inevitable when the new organisation had yet to set its course and establish the limits of its territory. Although almost as momentous as the formation of the Conservancy forty years previously, the new organisation in 1992 was very different. Gone, alas, was the freedom of individuals to take real innovative initiatives. Gone also, a rather narrow approach to nature conservation alone, and gone, the ease with which wrong routes could be taken or fanciful explorations made along interesting side roads, even at the highest levels. It took quite a lot of getting used to for the staff of both the previous organisations.

In 1992, Collier, the Chief Warden for the North-West and the Reserve's direct link to the Regional Office, moved to another post and Taylor became an Area Officer. The following year Lindsay also retired, after nineteen years at Beinn Eighe, for which he was awarded the MBE. Despite all these changes staff commitment remained high. Visitors to the Visitor Centre were holding at around 10,000 annually, while in 1993 and 1994 occupied bed-nights at the Field Station and Farmhouse, the only two years both were available, were 3800 and 3200 respectively, half of whom were volunteers. These volunteers, both the short term visits of parties from the Scottish Conservation Projects Trust (formerly the Conservation Corps and British Trust for Conservation Volunteers) and the long-term volunteers, were essential to the Reserve staff in keeping up the nursery and tree planting. Over the autumn of 1993 and the spring of 1994, the reduced workforce still managed to keep the woodland restoration programme going, planting 3870 broadleaved trees and 7180 Scots pine within the Ring Fence: the lower numbers being a reflection of a return to planting by minimum intervention. Nor was there a significant fall-off in monitoring and research. Surveys in 1993 and 1994 indicated that, although the browsing level by red deer in the ancient woodland was still too high, regeneration of the woodland was in a healthy state, both in the open areas of Coille na Glas Leitir and on the peripheries of the woodland remnants in the three gorges now within the Ring Fence.

Research during this period included work on the effects of trampling by visitors on the prostrate juniper heath by the Mountain Trail, assessment of the viability of pine seed and of the use of aerial photographs in measuring change in the woodland canopy. David Balharry, the son of the second Warden, completed his PhD thesis on the pine marten in the Loch Maree basin including the Reserve, carrying on the study of pine martens where his father had left off. His findings indicated that pine martens at Beinn Eighe were at a lower density and that the males had larger home ranges than in the Central Highlands of Scotland, an indication of the need for larger areas of mature pine wood in the west.

With the advent of Scottish Natural Heritage and its broader responsibilities for access and recreation, attention at Beinn Eighe, as well as on all other Reserves in Scotland, turned further towards the needs of visitors. In the 1960s Beinn Eighe had led the way in Britain in the reception of visitors to a Reserve, with its Trails and with its large and bold NNR signs, carved by Anderson-Bickley from fallen pine logs. In the 1990s this pioneering work was recognised by the interpretive staff of Scottish Natural Heritage, particularly John Walters, who was to commit more and more of his time to Beinn Eighe once it became one of the priority Reserves for the development of new Scottish Natural Heritage threshold signs. In 1995 a brief was prepared for an Interpretive Plan, automatic people counters were installed on the Trails and in the car park, and the new SNH threshold signs were designed and erected on the road approaches to the Reserve.

The new signs were very sophisticated and at a couple of metres tall and at 4.5 m in length – far larger and more eye-catching than the previous self-effacing Conservancy signs – large enough, in fact, to frighten traditionalists, just as had Balharry's thirty years before! At last, the signs gave the impression that here was somewhere special, a Reserve of status of which Scots should be proud and which caught the imagination of visitors. They immediately had a very positive impact on the visitors and numbers to the Information Centre rose to 14,000 in 1995 and then to 16,900 in 1996. Subsequent decreases in the late 1990s reflected tourism changes throughout Scotland generally. The Trail counters too showed that in the later years of the 1990s around 12,500 people annually used the Woodland Trail and around 7500 the Mountain Trail. The car park counters, however, also showed that a sizeable minority of those using the car park still did not actually walk one of the Trails. Many visitors are content to just to take in the information from the interpretive boards and leaflets and sit by the beautiful banks of Loch Maree.

Better days

The middle years of the 1990s represented yet another turning point for Beinn Eighe and other Scottish Reserves through their rehabilitation to the front rank of Scottish Natural Heritage's aims, but it took several years to get the Reserve back on a more positive and productive course. Clifford left in 1995 to be replaced as Reserve Manager by David Miller, who remains in that post in 2001. In the same year Peter Crichton, previously a tree surgeon, arrived as a permanent Site Management Officer (replacing the old Estate Worker grade). He took over the nursery work and oversaw the revolution in its management begun in Lindsay's time. In 1996, Maclean became the Deputy Reserve Manager. Three years later, Terry Doe, who had previously been an Estate Worker, but who had left to further his studies at Inverness College, was reappointed, this time as the second permanent Site Management Officer with particular responsibility for stalking. Outwith his Reserve responsibilities Doe is presently the Training Officer for the local Mountain Rescue Team. At this point the Reserve staff complement returned to the level of four permanent staff, equivalent to levels seven years earlier and prior to the formation of Scottish Natural Heritage. At the same time a Review of National Nature Reserves, started by Scottish Natural Heritage in 1992, was beginning to take shape. For the first time, using a careful selection of their main attributes, Reserves were to be measured and assessed, resulting in a league table. Beinn Eighe waited confidently to see where it would be placed.

Beinn Eighe had won its Council of Europe Diploma award in 1983, renewing it in 1988 and again in 1992, and had used the award to lever additional funds over the years. However, it was the third renewal in 1997 that was perhaps the most significant in terms of its timing. Firstly, it occurred in the year the Scottish Office reduced Scottish Natural Heritage's budget by 10 per cent with inevitable knock-

Visitors
in the Trails car park
by Loch Maree.
Photo: SNH

on reductions of funds to Reserve management. Secondly, it coincided with the introduction of new European funds. These funds were successfully tapped in 1996 when £66,000, in addition to funds from the local Enterprise Company and Scottish Natural Heritage, was used to carry out repairs to the Mountain Trail and to completely remodel and update the Trails car park. Thirdly, it happened to coincide with the introduction of a European Directive on the protection of natural and semi-natural habitats that, just as with the Wildlife and the Countryside Act 1981, stretched the organisation's staffing resources.

The Directive required European Community countries to designate Special Areas of Conservation (SAC) for particular habitats and species that were rare in a European context. It also required positive management, if necessary, to bring these into a healthy state. In a British context Beinn Eighe is a very important site for a number of these threatened habitats, including the Caledonian forest, several types of moorland heaths from the boreal climate at the foot of the mountain to the alpine near the summit and the fern communities of the quartzite screes and cliffs.

The 1996 report of the assessor for the European Council, Jan Lundqvist (of the Swedish Environmental Protection Agency), spoke highly of various aspects of the Reserve management, particularly drawing attention to the record of 243 separate research projects to date and concluding with: 'In my opinion the state of conservation of Beinn Eighe NNR now is even higher than in 1992, when I carried out my previous on-the-spot appraisal.' This was a tremendous endorsement of the effort of local staff over those years, especially considering that in the same years some European Diploma sites had been deselected as they had failed to meet the conditions. The renewal of the Diploma, the new expertise required of staff to draw up the highly technical paperwork necessary for the SAC designation and to obtain European funding, plus the Reserve Review, no doubt all helped to re-secure the fourth permanent post on the Reserve.

Management plans

The content and structure of a Reserve Management Plan are not just a record of management aims and their justifications, but a fascinating insight into the attitudes of the organisation to conservation management at the time they are written. The 1957 Plan was a very basic document following the structure laid down by Nicholson, the Director General at the time. The second Plan in 1967 developed that structure and extended the aims of the Reserve, but it lacked some rigour, allowing the woodland restoration programme to drift off course for a long period culminating in the 1990 Plan. This Management Plan set out to re-establish first principles and to firmly base new objectives on a thorough analysis and a strict rationale, following a very detailed Conservancy format. The format was developed in an attempt to bring all Reserve Plans into line and to encourage Reserve Wardens to prioritise their work, plan ahead and make clear present and future costs. It was also designed to make use of new computer technology and every conceivable task, large or small, was therefore coded. It is a very logical, but a rather weighty document, that is not easily digestible. The fourth and last Management Plan to date, for the period 1995–2005, is a slightly simpler version of its predecessor. Its main aims for the natural environment are much the same as they have always been, except that all the plant communities and species, and not just the Caledonian forest, are equally identified as needing conservation and enhancement management. The differences between the aims of the two reflect the new responsibilities of Scottish Natural Heritage. The 1995 Plan is the first to acknowledge that it must take the landscape and the archaeology of the Reserve into account in management. It is also the first to identify explicitly that there should be: '…provision for … the demonstration of best practice', in addition to the provision of education and training. It is also the first Plan to aim 'To maintain good relations with the local community, and where appropriate develop local involvement with the Reserve.'

Woodland restoration comes of age

Apart from substantial plantings of exotic tree species and Scots pine of unknown origin in the Forestry Commission enclosure and large numbers of Glen Affric pine in the penultimate two, there were only two other enclosures planted with non-local pine in the late 1950s. One of those was very straightforward, as all the 1711 pines were known to be of Glen Affric origin, so they were all felled. The other was not so straightforward. Here, the records suggested that only 170 of the 1170 Scots pines were of Glen Affric origin and they might have been left. This enclosure was situated in Glen Torridon, right opposite the West Coulin native pine wood and the Glen Affric trees had to be removed as the Commission were unwilling to recognise the West Coulin native pine wood as a registered Scots pine seed collection area until the pines were felled. Because it was not known exactly where the Glen Affric seed had been planted in this enclosure, all the trees were felled in 1992.

These smaller enclosures, however, were relatively easy to deal with as far as the removal of non-local Scots pine was concerned: either numbers were relatively few or the trees relatively small. It was what to do with the Forestry Commission enclosure that proved a headache. This was a relatively large at 125 ha, thirty-year-old, commercial plantation of 50,000 non-local Scots pine, lodgepole pine and Sitka spruce, and a rather obvious, though unwanted (by the Conservancy) landscape feature. By 1988, although separately fenced, it was effectively within the Ring Fence and, unfortunately, the well-grown and thick woodland harboured red, roe and even sika deer. It was the worst of both worlds, for both deer and tree seed leaked into the Ring Fence area. On the one hand deer began to cause damage to the new plantings being made within the Ring Fence and on the other, non-local Scots pine, lodgepole and Sitka began to germinate and grow.

For a number of years management was limited to a regular cull of deer within the Forestry Commission enclosure and uprooting regenerating trees within the Ring Fence. At first, when funds and staff were at low ebb, it was thought that all the trees might gradually be removed in small coupes over a fifty-year period. This had the advantage of minimising the landscape impact compared to removing the whole thing in one go. However, it did not address the issues of the small deer population or the regenerating non-local pine that would simply carry on over this period. When Miller arrived in the mid-1990s, in the absence of in-house commercial forest expertise, he brought in a silvicultural adviser who recommended felling the trees in three coupes over a ten-year period. Once again, the purpose of this was to lessen the landscape impact: the local community having been consulted and expressed some concern at the felling of such a large numbers of trees. However, this only extended the length of time that both deer and regenerating trees would be a problem and continue to take up valuable staff time. Finally, the bullet was bitten in 2000 when a start was made, under a Forestry Commission Woodland Grant Scheme, to remove the whole plantation in one process, which should be completed in 2001. The Scheme ensures that the felled trees will be replaced over time by both planted and regenerating local native tree species, while carrying out the felling all at once eliminates both the deer and the non-native tree regeneration issues at a stroke. To explain its reasons for removing the plantation, since the loss of such a large area of trees might reflect badly on Scottish Natural Heritage, an informative and interpretive board was erected adjacent to the fence, on the side of the Torridon road. Coincidentally, and rather ironically after years of Scottish Natural Heritage concern at the impact such management might have, Coulin Estate, on the opposite side of the same road, started a similar Scheme, but on a *very* much larger plantation.

Over the years there has been a heavy loss of planted broadleaved trees, sometimes due to poor planting technique or planting in inappropriate soils and to their attraction of marauding deer. But before we lay too much blame on the many volunteer planters we must remember that a lot of planting could not have taken place without their help. It is also likely that most of the loss has been due to the very poor quality soils in the first place. This high loss rate is slowly being overcome at Beinn Eighe through the development of new nursery techniques. Up to 1990 trees were planted 'bare-rooted': that is just prior to planting, they were lifted from the earth of the transplant lines in the nursery, put in a bag, taken to the hill and then slipped into a cutting made with a spade.

The root system therefore went straight from the relatively benign soil in the nursery to the very acid and nutrient-poor soil on the hill. After 1990 the staff at Beinn Eighe began to experiment with 'root-trainers'. Using this technique the seedling is grown on within a plug of compost in a plastic cell or root-trainer, and the whole plug is planted with the tree on the hill. The root system is therefore always enclosed by soil and does not have to suffer the shock of being removed from one soil to another. However, in the early 1990s the nursery management

David Miller
holding Scots pine seedlings
in root-trainers in poly-tunnel.
Photo: N. Benvie / SNH

system still used outside seedbeds, transplant lines and only a small number of root-trainers. Constant irrigation of the root-trainers by hand was time consuming and the whole process still extended over a couple of years. There was still some way to go.

Since the mid-1990s techniques in the nursery have taken a quantum leap forward. All tree seedlings are now grown under a poly-tunnel, from germination until removal outside for hardening off. The rate of success of germination and growth within pots under polythene is so high that pine can now be germinated in the spring and planted the following year – a third of the time it took previously, while birch can now be germinated and planted in the same year. There is no longer any need for the previous laborious outdoor tasks of weeding and transplanting, often under attack from midges, nor to plan two years or more ahead. Today, even the irrigation of the fibrous pots is being fully automated. Another advantage of using individual pots is the opportunity to control the medium in which the seed and seedling are grown. This allows the nursery manager to use a medium approaching the acidity of the soil of the hill, thereby further lessening the shock of the final planting. Casual observation already indicates that trees grown and planted under the modern system have a greater chance of survival and show better growth than those treated traditionally. The future of tree planting on Beinn Eighe will therefore be much less time-consuming, more efficient and more successful than in the past.

The planting rate within the Ring Fence, by the turn of the millennium, was of the order of 15,000 trees annually: substantially less than when trees were planted on ploughed ground, but the results are now something much closer to natural regeneration. Very soon, as the most suitable ground within the Ring Fence is planted up, the need for even those numbers will decline. Planting will then be limited to beating-up, filling in smaller and smaller niches. More trees will perhaps be given away to good causes and if the nursery's future is to match its illustrious past, the Reserve will have to look elsewhere for new homes for its native trees, perhaps The National Trust for Scotland property at Torridon and neighbouring private estates.

Prior to the erection of the Ring Fence in 1988, excluding the Forestry Commission enclosure and the non-local provenance Scots pine that have been, or are to be felled; some 280,000 native trees had been planted in the various enclosures erected from 1954. By far the majority of these are Scots pines, while the minority are made up of a variety of broadleaved trees. Since the completion of the Ring Fence the pace has been sustained with more than 100,000 trees planted, comprising approximately 50 per cent Scots pine, 20 per cent birch and 30 per cent of a further twelve species of trees and shrubs. In total, therefore, over the fifty-year period, very nearly 400,000 native trees have been planted on Beinn Eighe.

The result of all this planting, even allowing for all the trials and errors, has been the achievement of the original aims for restoration and extension of the ancient pine wood. Coille na Glas Leitir is regenerating and the most suitable parts of the remainder of the low ground have been planted up with the first generation of a new forest. How those visionaries of the 1940s would rejoice if they could see it now! There is no doubt that it has taken much longer than many would have wished, despite McVean's warning way back in the early

Tree planter on the hill
with Scots pines in root-trainers.
Photo: SNH

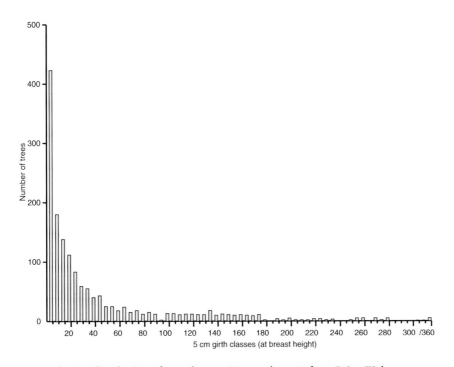

Fig 13 **The size distribution of sample trees** (*Pinus sylvestris*) **from Beinn Eighe native woodland in 1990 (Clifford 1991). See Fig 2 Clifford 1997.**

1950s that it would take a long time. However, it must be remembered that trees are long-lived and that natural regeneration does not need to be rapid in order to secure the continuity of woodland. That the incredible effort of so many people has been so successful is evident in the age-distribution curve (Fig 13) for Scots pine in the native woodland on Beinn Eighe. It now looks very healthy and very different to that drawn up by McVean for Coille na Glas Leitir in 1953 (see Fig 5).

A new approach to the red deer cull

Following the closure of the Ring Fence in 1988, the increased level of the deer cull continued through until 1991, principally in and around Coille na Glas Leitir. However, the long-term monitoring transects in the ancient woodland revealed in 1992 that there were still unacceptably high levels of browsing on the regenerating trees. The 1993 cull level was therefore raised once again, but at the same time staff readdressed the factors governing the level of the cull within the Reserve and a proposal was mooted that in future, cull levels should be directly related to the level of their impact on the regenerating trees. A deer count in 1996 indicated that there were approximately 2.4 deer per 100 ha over the whole Reserve. However, half of these were counted in or at the edge of the ancient woodland at a density of 29 per 100 ha, far too high for successful regeneration. The cull was therefore raised again. Today in 2001, deer numbers are around 130 at a density close to 2.6 per 100 ha. This is just below the generally accepted figure of three per 100 ha that would allow natural regeneration of woodland and extraordinarily, it is almost exactly the density proposed by Darling in 1951.

Since then, counts of deer droppings, sample counts by stalkers and observations of browsing damage in the ancient woodland have governed the level of cull. Traditional selective culling ceased some time ago and now the one-sixth cull, initiated in the 1960s, has also come to an end. There are of course advantages of an optimum number of deer in regenerating woodland, such as the creation of niches in thick ground vegetation for seedling germination through trampling and a more diverse pattern and distribution of trees and shrubs through browsing. Even the great Gaelic poet and stalker, Duncan Ban MacIntyre, knew in the eighteenth century that here was where red deer truly belonged. Nevertheless, although the level of deer grazing may be the optimum for regenerating woodland, it may not be appropriate for high-level grasslands and moorland. This was recognised in the 1995 Plan, with the result that monitoring of these and other plant communities has continued in order to assess the impact of grazing at present deer numbers. It may well be that grazing levels on these communities are also too high.

The very last deer fence to be erected to date at Beinn Eighe was put up with the agreement of the owner and occupier of Taagan in 1999. This fence is intended to protect Coille na Glas Leitir from deer that cross the river from the Letterewe and Kinlochewe Forests. A glance at the OS Landranger map will show that there is very little woodland left on the southeasterly-facing slopes above the river and Loch Maree: nothing like there must have been prior to the ironworks in the seventeenth century. The general lack of woodland shelter concentrates deer in the remaining ancient remnants, in the winter months especially, and it is one of the principal reasons for their lack of regeneration and continuing decline, not just in Wester Ross, but also all over the Highlands. Prior to the erection of the fence the last deer count solely for Coille na Glas Leitir was eighty-seven in 1996, but a count in December 2000 found only forty-nine: the fence appears to be doing its job. On another corner of the Reserve in Glen Torridon, neighbours are putting up new fencing as part of a new Scots pine-planting scheme under a Native Woodland grant from the Forestry Commission. The additional fencing and concomitant reduction of deer there should assist with the easing of deer pressure on this part of the Reserve. The future therefore looks good for the Beinn Eighe woodland.

However, after fifty years of deer control on the Reserve and more than thirty years of co-operation within the Gairloch Conservation Unit area, there is still conflict between the aims of the Reserve and its surrounding private landowners. John Wills, who bought Grudie Estate, immediately to the west, from Mrs Greig in 1965, manages his deer for sport stalking, but some of these same deer cross into Coille na Glas Leitir in the winter for the same reasons that Letterewe and Kinlochewe deer cross the river at Taagan. Wills welcomes the walkers and climbers who regularly cross his Estate to reach the Beinn Eighe ridge, some of whom are attracted to the area by the Reserve publicity, but he does not like to see *his* deer being culled on the Reserve. It is undesirable, impractical and probably too expensive to erect a deer fence between the two properties, but in the absence of sufficient woodland shelter on Grudie, some deer will continue to cross the boundary. The pursuit of the 'good neighbour' policy has been an important factor in the management of Reserves since the origin of the Nature Conservancy. At Beinn Eighe this has largely continued through the Gairloch Conservation Unit and occasional direct contact. As long as management aims differ across Estate boundaries, however, there are bound to be differences of opinion, but the Reserve *has* helped create a forum for discussion of these differences. Lest we have given the impression that these meetings are always confrontational, the closing words of the minutes of the October GCU meeting in 2000 should be reassuring: 'Seamus MacNally was thanked for hosting the meeting and providing a fine selection of biscuits.' Seamus MacNally is The National Trust for Scotland Ranger at Torridon and nephew of the previous Ranger Lea MacNally.

Visitors and residents

In 1996 the original Farmhouse and Warden's house that had accommodated long-term volunteers were converted to offices for Reserve and Area staff. This was a very welcome improvement on the portacabin that had been used as an office for several years, but it also meant a reduction in the available space for the long-term volunteers who made up around 50 per cent of the volunteer workforce. These young men and women, often placements from college and universities, come from all over Europe and occasionally farther afield. They are provided with basic waterproof gear and free accommodation in return for working a five-day week on the Reserve. However, even with the reduction in accommodation the level of contribution from long-term volunteers in 1999 remained steady at around 1000 days. The other main contributors to voluntary effort on the Reserve were the Scottish Conservation Projects Trust and the Scottish Wildlife Trust; support from the former, particularly in nursery and tree planting work, stretches right back to the early 1960s, but in recent years the latter has been more prominent on the Reserve. Beinn Eighe has also traditionally provided opportunities in nature conservation work to those of less advantaged backgrounds such as the boys from the Young Offenders Institution at Polmont. More recently this opportunity has been extended to include disabled people, groups of whom have made very successful visits to Beinn Eighe in the late 1990s. The Reserve also has a long tradition of taking on training of the unemployed. There have been three very successful placements under the Government's New Deal initiative for the long-term unemployed in the last few years – a great improvement on the Manpower Services scheme twenty years previously. As with the long-term volunteers, these young people are provided with accommodation, in this case for six months, during which time they receive training in conservation management and effectively become paid Reserve management staff.

The knock-on effect of losing accommodation through the creation of the new offices and having to accommodate volunteers in the Field Station was reduced space for the students carrying out research and survey on the Reserve. Nevertheless, in 1999 the Reserve still managed to accommodate eight students carrying out projects ranging from geological mapping to habitat surveys, while fifteen reports were produced on subjects such as deer parasites, assessment of

Tim Clifford addresses
Norwegian foresters
in Coille na Glas Leitir.
Photo: SNH

grazing and trampling impacts on the Gairloch Conservation Unit area, the relationship between prostrate and upright juniper, the monitoring of one rare lichen and the distribution of another.

A substantial piece of research work published in 1997 owed at least one of its origins to Beinn Eighe and continued a now established tradition of 'old boys' returning to become administrators or contributors to the further understanding of the wildlife of the area. Jeff Watson first came to Beinn Eighe in 1967 with a school party from Edinburgh. In 1981, this time in the role of a research worker on the Nature Conservancy Council's Chief Scientist's Team, he returned to pick up on the earlier work of Lockie and Balharry on the distribution of golden eagles. Thirty years after his initial visit he published a comprehensive monograph, *The Golden Eagle* (1997). Today, coincidentally, Watson is Scottish Natural Heritage's Director for the North Area, including Beinn Eighe.

Researcher carrying out beetle survey on Scots pine.
Photo: D. Miller

Coincidentally, another wildlife study in the area, this time initiated by Cross, introduced Greg Mudge, Scottish Natural Heritage's present Area Manager for North-West Scotland, to Beinn Eighe. The Reserve abuts Loch Maree and, despite the Conservancy's early interest in its native greylag geese, the real wildlife feature of this loch is its black-throated diver population. Cross's pioneering work surveying and monitoring this population was taken up by Mudge prior to his joining the Conservancy in the 1980s. Mudge was then involved in building nesting rafts for the birds which proved to be so successful that they are still in use. The black-throated diver population of Loch Maree is by far the largest and most studied population in Britain and the birds are so regularly seen that Scottish Natural Heritage is now planning to provide illustrated information on them at the Trails car park from which they can regularly be viewed in the breeding season.

In the same year as the publication of Watson's book, Miller initiated one of the most interesting and valuable pieces of work on Beinn Eighe, when he contracted a local Gaelic scholar, Roy Wentworth, to draw up a list of Gaelic place-names on Beinn Eighe (*Summary of Gaelic Place-Names on Beinn Eighe NNR*, 1998). The result of this project, which took Wentworth in search of many old documents and to the homes of nearly all the native residents of the area around Beinn Eighe, is an invaluable record of 240 Gaelic place-names. Many old names have already disappeared, but those that remain, now safeguarded forever by this work, are keys to the understanding of place and use. They add another dimension to understanding and managing Beinn Eighe and the work reflects Scottish Natural Heritage's wider role compared to its predecessor bodies. A new map of the area has been produced and is unique in recording and making available the numerous Gaelic names for so many of the landscape features, living names that have been handed down through generations of local people.

The Reserve and the community

The relationship between the Reserve and the village has waxed and waned over the years. First impressions often linger and Beinn Eighe's new owner in 1951 appeared to represent one more estate owner managing the land for purposes unconnected with the villagers or their way of life. There is a certain regret on both sides now for the initial lack of effort to forge mutually beneficial links, such as accessing the experience and knowledge of generations of local hill managers in exchange for the science and practice of conservation management. This was a form of blindness that affected the Conservancy on almost all the Reserves established at that time. The barriers gradually came down through the 1960s and 1970s as Kinlochewe residents became more involved in the events of the Reserve and vice versa, and local people were employed on the Reserve.

Over the next twenty years the relationship remained little changed. The Conservancy got on with the management of the Reserve and occasionally officially informed the village community what it was doing. Unofficially, of course, there was daily communication between Kinlochewe residents and Reserve staff who lived locally and sent their children to the local school. Outwith the Reserve, particularly with the advent of Scottish Natural Heritage in 1992, grants became available for school and conservation projects and the staff made specific efforts to ensure that the village benefited. Whenever there was a reason for celebration the Reserve held an open day and invited the community to Anancaun.

There was one event in February 1985, however, that illustrates the very real bond of mutual interest that has come to exist between the Reserve and the Kinlochewe community. A bonfire in a garden in Kinlochewe leaped the road and swept on to the Reserve, threatening Coille na Glas Leitir. Led by Cross, the Reserve staff, Forestry Commission workers from Slattadale Forest and nearly all the men of the village turned out to fight the fire and eventually succeeded in putting it out. Clifford recalls returning from a visit to Inverness to find the fire at its height and immediately joining in the fire-fighting. He found himself standing shoulder-to-shoulder with the village shopkeeper on the freezing ground, filthy with cinders, and realising that the latter must have sprinted straight from home without second thought as he was still wearing his best black leather shoes.

The invitation to community representatives – local Councillor Roy MacIntyre and Community Council representatives Malcolm MacDonald and Elinor Wallace – to attend the Reserve Management Advisory Group in 1998 was therefore not only a very significant, but also a very appropriate, step towards a real involvement of the Kinlochewe community in the management of the

Schoolchildren at Kinlochewe Primary with their Beinn Eighe 50th birthday poster.
Photo: J. MacPherson / SNH

Reserve. It ensures an official and regular opportunity for the people of Kinlochewe to put across their views on the management of the Reserve and for Scottish Natural Heritage to seek the community's opinion on any developments it might plan.

The following year the staff at Beinn Eighe, supported by their colleagues from Inverness and others including The National Trust for Scotland, organised an Open Day at Anancaun especially for the local community. Fliers were hand delivered to every house in Kinlochewe, Achnasheen and Torridon, posters were put up and an advertisement inserted in the local paper. The purpose was to welcome the communities, to provide a day out for families and to explain and demonstrate the management of the Reserve. Hands-on activities were organised for the children. Among many activities, there were guided walks, tours of the nursery, deer stalking with camera, a mini-beast display and tree seedlings were given away. It was a satisfying success attracting on a rather poor summer day 150 people, half of whom were children.

New funds, new life

The late 1990s, as well as marking the first official involvement of the local community in the management of Beinn Eighe, was a very busy period for the Reserve and Area staff with the preparation of plans and justifications for improvement to all aspects of visitor management, partly in connection with the Reserve's approaching fiftieth anniversary. Firstly, extensive repairs and upgrading were carried out on the Coire nan Laoigh and Allt à Chùirn footpaths: the main accesses to the Beinn Eighe ridge. Secondly, a brief was prepared for a total revamp of visitor facilities at Aultroy, which had remained unchanged since Taylor improved the interpretation in 1984/5. Thirdly, a bid for funds to complete repairs to the Mountain Trail was prepared, and fourthly, under the terms of the last renewal of the European Diploma in 1997, plans for a new Reserve leaflet were drawn up. The Visitor Centre and Mountain Trail projects, particularly, were going to be comprehensive and very expensive and required detailed justifications in order to win the approval of senior management. The total package of facilities, when completed, will stand alongside the creation of the Mountain Trail and Aultroy Visitor Centre, and the refurbishments of the Field Station and Farmhouse, as yet another great milestone in the development of Beinn Eighe National Nature Reserve.

At this point Beinn Eighe emerged from Scottish Natural Heritage's Reserve Review with flying colours. In future, the Review stated, Reserves will have to satisfy four attributes: primacy of nature in management, best management practice, national importance and surety of long-term objectives. Beinn Eighe is owned by Scottish Natural Heritage, has a long history of good management, is internationally important and therefore meets the attributes. Reserves must also serve at least one of three purposes: national awareness, specialised management and research. Once again Beinn Eighe had fulfilled all these objectives. In fact, Beinn Eighe could rightly say that it had been satisfying the attributes and meeting the objectives longer than any other Reserve in Britain. This accolade in recognition of the Reserve's high-quality management perhaps won at least half the battle in terms of obtaining funds.

Ross & Cromarty Footpath Trust Board check the quality of work by their footpath workers at Coire an Laiogh.
Photo: D. Miller

Restoration of the Mountain Trail was estimated to require in the region of £90,000 over a period of three years. During this period it is intended to repair it to such a high standard that it will require only minimum maintenance over the next ten years. This may seem a very large sum of money for a single project on a Reserve but it has to be measured against a previous history of thirty years of continuous repair at an average annual cost of £3000: in 1987 alone 1000 volunteer days were given to working on the Trail. The principal reason why there had to be continual annual maintenance was that much of these repairs had been carried out by unskilled volunteers and did not last. Modern standards of health and safety are much tougher than they were and if the Mountain Trail is to remain open and safe for public use, what is now needed is a professional job that *will* last.

The Mountain Trail is the only high-level, self-guided walk in Britain. Every year it attracts in the region of 10,000 walkers of all ages. One of the many testaments from visitors simply says: 'My family and I walked the Mountain Trail on Beinn Eighe near Loch Maree last week and were amazed at the care, work and dedication that had been put in to making it possible … it is a magnificent walk.' The decision on whether or not to fund the necessary repair had serious implications for the standing of Scottish Natural Heritage in the area and there were fears locally that the Mountain Trail might have to close. The case went all the way to the SNH Chief Executive, Roger Crofts who approved the funding for its repair with the words: 'It is clear … that the Beinn Eighe Mountain Trail is an important part of the visitor structure in Wester Ross', so assuring the future of this unique asset to conservation. The work began in 2001 and completion is planned for the end of 2002.

The bid for the Beinn Eighe NNR Visitor Centre at Aultroy has been very much more ambitious, but unlike previous efforts this time it has had a much greater input from interpretive staff from the Inverness office. In fact Walters, who had been involved with Beinn Eighe interpretation since he had joined the Nature Conservancy Council in 1986, now took the lead on the new interpretive work. Like the Mountain Trail, the Visitor Centre had been a first in its day, but it had been refurbished only once since it first opened in 1974. By 1996 it was felt that additional self-guiding trails were required for visitors, but that these should start from the Visitor Centre itself and should include provision for disabled people. The new plan for Aultroy represents a radical move away from the normal conception of information centres and trails. The trails will be interactive, will be inside and outside and of varying length, in order to give those who cannot get into the ancient woodland of Coille na Glas Leitir or up the mountain of Beinn Eighe, a taste of those experiences. The total cost will be nearly £0.5 million and will be shared between Scottish Natural Heritage, the Heritage Lottery Fund and Ross and Cromarty Enterprise, with additional funding from the European Community. The finished product should be a fitting addition to, and recognition of, the national and international importance of Britain's first National Nature Reserve and the contribution it has made in introducing the British public to the natural heritage over many years. It will also continue to be of substantial benefit to the communities of Kinlochewe and Wester Ross.

Walkers follow the Trail
through Coille na Glas Leitir.
Photo: SNH

10 Achievements and the future

> 'Beinn Eighe, along with The National Trust for Scotland's Torridon Estate, Loch Maree, Letterewe and Fisherfield, are the core of one of Scotland's most distinctive and prized landscapes. It is essential for the future, to sustain that landscape and the things that make it work: conservation, forestry, agricultural, visitor and sporting management, and that the people who live there can play their full part.'
>
> Roger Crofts
> Chief Executive, Scottish Natural Heritage
> 2001

The natural heritage

When Coille na Glas Leitir first came to the attention of the relevant Government committees in the 1940s, and when Beinn Eighe was purchased in 1951, none of those involved was aware of the true importance of its nature conservation and landscape features, nor how well known and regarded the area was to become. In purchasing Beinn Eighe in addition to Coille na Glas Leitir from a generous Mrs Greig, Berry secured for the nation what must have seemed like an enormous area of land with its range of climates and plant communities from boreal pine wood to summit moss heaths, of which many additional features have been found to be of international importance. Not only that, but Reserve status secured complete freedom of access to the great sweep of mountain peak, ridge and corrie for hill walkers and climbers, while through its public facilities it has made the experience of this landscape and its wildlife available to the general public.

To anyone unfamiliar with land management in the Highlands of Scotland, and unaware of the perceived conflict between traditional sporting, forestry or agricultural management and management for nature conservation and access, the importance of ownership in management is probably unclear. In fact, Scottish Natural Heritage's ownership of Beinn Eighe, on behalf of the people of Scotland, is probably one of the Reserve's most significant attributes. Generally speaking, National Nature Reserves are under lease or management agreement with private owners. Beinn Eighe Reserve is actually in the minority, there being only seventeen out of seventy-one Reserves in Scotland that are wholly owned by Scottish Natural Heritage. The total area owned by Scottish Natural Heritage is around 34,000 ha, and incidentally, if that seems a very large figure, it is just 1000 ha greater than the private estate of Letterewe on the opposite banks of Loch Maree from Beinn Eighe.

Ownership of Beinn Eighe has provided long-term security and allowed the sort of substantial investment that all the major conservation and restoration management projects required. Trees grow slowly to maturity, many beyond the lifetime of a single generation of people. Woodlands, with their characteristic soils, plants and animals, take very much longer, perhaps several thousand years. The foresight of those pioneers of early nature conservation in Britain did not end with the purchase of the land. There is no doubt that the further purchase of the farm buildings at Anancaun and Aultroy, outwith the Reserve, made possible all the future developments for the public, and research and voluntary contribution. The width of vision of the pioneers was the making of Beinn Eighe National Nature Reserve.

The thread that has run through this book has been the management of the ancient Coille na Glas Leitir and its restoration to areas where it is judged to have existed in the past and could still do so today. Initially, as we have seen, this was to be achieved by the most natural means possible and since there was little evidence of regeneration on its own, this implied some minimal intervention. In retrospect it is clear that ecological principles were compromised in the 1960s and 1970s in order to achieve rapid tree cover, albeit with the best of intentions That management policy came to a dead stop in 1980 because research led to the discovery and recognition of native tree provenances and to the uniqueness of the Wester Ross pine woods, in particular, now safeguarded at Beinn Eighe.

We who can now sit in judgement of mistakes that were made should remember two particular points. First, it was at least as much the Conservancy's ground-breaking and sometimes blind struggle towards establishing the ecological principles of woodland restoration at Beinn Eighe, as any other, that contributed to both the Forestry Commission's provenance policy in the late 1970s and its own at Beinn Eighe in the early 1980s. Second, we should rejoice that the Conservancy bought Coille na Glas Leitir in the first place, otherwise it is quite obvious from what happened in the Forestry Commission enclosure, that had Sir Beresford-Pierse and the Commission had their way all the low ground at Beinn Eighe would have been ploughed and blanket-planted with not only Scots pine of non Wester Ross provenance, but probably non-Scottish too with a good dash of Sitka spruce and lodgepole pine. It is almost unimaginable now how, in the 1980s, Coille na Glas Leitir could have been disentangled from such management.

For the last decade, woodland management at Beinn Eighe has followed two principles. Within the Ring Fence, in the absence of red deer, there has been no ploughing. Planting has been carried out with minimum soil disturbance, a mixture of native species appropriate to ground conditions and limited to those small areas judged to be able to support trees. Outwith the fence, in Coille na Glas Leitir, in the presence of a controlled population of red deer, natural regeneration has been allowed to proceed at its own pace without any interference. The Ring Fence is unlikely to remain deer proof for another ten years without increasingly expensive repairs. By that time, most of the plantings within will still be of a stature that will make them vulnerable to browsing. Because of sheer cost it is very unlikely that this fence will be replaced and, if it is not, the red deer population on Beinn Eighe as a whole, will have to be maintained at a level compatible with natural woodland regeneration. This level may have to be even lower if it is found that the mountain heaths and grasslands require it.

For all that has been said about the vagaries of woodland management over the first fifty years at Beinn Eighe, the immense effort invested by so many *has* resulted today in the fulfilment of the vision shared by Pearsall and others. Coille na Glas Leitir *is* regenerating and the germ of a future woodland *has* been established on the rest of the low ground of the Reserve. Neither should we forget that many of the basic principles for restoring native woodland in Scotland were established at Beinn Eighe: principles that have survived the passage of time and are still being applied. Nor have the lessons of error and failure been wasted, because now they can be avoided. The example is there at Beinn Eighe. Anyone taking the Woodland or Mountain Trails through this ancient remnant of Caledonian pine wood cannot fail to be impressed by its vibrancy and health. Walk up the footpath into Allt à Chùirn or the pony path into Allt Sguabaig among regenerating pines, or drive down the Glen Torridon road and look at the mixed plantings that are so slowly becoming established on the devastated southern slopes of the Reserve. Regeneration and growth of pine wood is a slow process in the climate of the north-west, but it has begun again at Beinn Eighe at last, after an interval of at least 200 years.

How many deer is too many deer?

Deer management policy at Beinn Eighe has now settled at a population level compatible with natural tree regeneration. This approach to deer management, now being practised increasingly across Scotland, notably at Creag Meagaidh, Abernethy, Mar Lodge and other National Trust for Scotland properties, but on very few private estates, has turned deer management on its head. Its fundamental question is no longer how many deer are wanted, but how many deer can the land sustain while allowing restoration of its natural potential? Sites like Beinn Eighe will one day demonstrate, even to those whose heads are buried deep in the peat, that the proper balance of red deer to their natural environment will result in a return to the magnificent and productive animals that they must have been in the not-too-distant past, as well as the diverse and productive environment in which they lived.

In 1967, Beinn Eighe was the first place in Scotland to recognise that deer management could not be carried out in isolation from neighbouring estates and so the surrounding estate owners were brought together to form the Gairloch Conservation Unit (GCU), the first Deer Management Group in Scotland. The first count of deer on the GCU area in 1967 gave a count of 1563 in total. Numbers appear to have reached a peak the following year at 1625, since when

Coille na Glas Leitir from above the position of the very first enclosure. Taken from the same position as Robert Adam's photograph in 1930 (see page 28). Natural regeneration is a lengthy process!
Photo: T. Clifford

they have remained at around 1000 animals. Since both the Conservancy and The National Trust for Scotland have reduced their deer populations by more than 200 and since, through the erection of enclosures, fairly large areas of land have now been excluded from deer grazing, the apparent reduction in deer numbers throughout the GCU area is probably not significant. The deer density per unit area therefore has probably not changed significantly in thirty years. In contrast, deer numbers in many places elsewhere in Scotland are, sadly, still increasing.

While the GCU area has one of the lowest densities of deer in the Highlands, at around three per 100 ha, most of its ground represents some of the poorest grazing in the Highlands. To the credit of GCU deer managers they have not tried to keep their deer numbers unnaturally high, either by supplementary feeding of stags in winter or artificially fertilising grassland to provide better feeding. Although present density may not seem far off that needed for natural regeneration of the woodland in the GCU area it has to be remembered that in winter deer selectively seek shelter and food in the scraps of remnant woodlands,

A visitor checks his information at the foot of the Pony Path.
Photo: J. MacPherson / SNH

just as in Coille na Glas Leitir. Low-ground, with its woodland remnants, is less than two-thirds of the total GCU area, so deer density in these areas probably increases to more than ten per 100 ha in the winter season; at least triple the density that would allow natural regeneration of the remnant woodlands. The GCU is one of only a handful of the sixty or so Deer Management Groups that is now progressing a management plan and it is to be hoped that it might build on its good management record, reduce deer densities to allow the restoration of deer's natural woodland and scrub habitat.

Although the Gairloch Conservation Unit neither became the co-ordinated land management unit Boyd had envisaged, nor to date, reduced overall deer numbers compatible with restoration of the environment, it has, for more than thirty years, provided a very useful discussion forum for Beinn Eighe and its neighbours. Some of its members, The National Trust for Scotland at Torridon, and the estate of Gairloch and Conon, as well as the adjacent Coulin Estate, have taken up Native Pinewood schemes with grant support from the Forestry Commission and some very large areas of land will now be restored to native woodland. These will, of course, be fenced so that deer numbers can be kept up for sporting purposes outwith the growing woodlands. It is perhaps too much to have hoped that the estates would have carried out woodland restoration in the absence of fencing, but at least it is a step in the right direction. Who knows, as traditions change, where the Gairloch Conservation Unit might be in another half-century or what part it might play in the future co-ordinated management of this area of Wester Ross?

Anancaun and Aultroy

Over the Reserve's fifty–year life, the Field Station at Anancaun has recorded literally thousands of occupied bed-nights. These represent hundreds of individual volunteers from schoolchildren, students and postgraduates to non-

Tourist traffic
passing Visitor Centre sign
on the Loch Maree road.
Photo: J. MacPherson / SNH

academics and special needs groups. Many of these have experienced their very first taste of remoteness, wilderness and countryside management at Beinn Eighe. Many have also sought out Beinn Eighe deliberately as part of academic or vocational courses. Discussing their time at Beinn Eighe with those who have been volunteers in the past, it is clear that the experience brought a greater understanding of nature conservation management and sowed a seed of empathy for wildlife that was not there before and that has stayed with them for the rest of their lives.

It is impossible to evaluate the contribution Beinn Eighe has made to enrich these lives, nor the influence these people have brought to bear for the cause of the natural environment. However, by any measure, Beinn Eighe's achievement in this context is one that very few other Reserves can match. The efforts of the volunteers have amounted to the equivalent of at least two additional full-time staff for every year of the Reserve. This has been of immense benefit, particularly in times of limited funds or staff shortages.

Like all Reserves, Beinn Eighe commissions specific research or surveys from specialists. A great deal of the less specialist biological work, however, has been accomplished by students, often through third year, honours or postgraduate dissertations. They have contributed a very impressive list of scientific papers that have added so much to our knowledge and understanding of the geology and ecology of Beinn Eighe. It is difficult to evaluate the contribution of students when adding up the balance sheet of annual costs and benefits of their projects, but as with the contribution of volunteers, mutual benefits extend beyond the paperwork, much farther in time and distance than can ever appear in any report or evaluation. In addition, the work commissioned by Miller from Wentworth on Gaelic place-names, in its own way, is ground-breaking. Perhaps for the first time the Government body responsible for the countryside has recognised that local cultural heritage, which is inextricably linked to historical land management, is a natural partner of the natural heritage.

The year of Beinn Eighe's fiftieth anniversary will see the completion of restoration work to the Mountain Trail, surely one of the most ambitious, impressive and successful self-guided trails in Europe. There is certainly nothing comparable in the British Isles. It is wonderfully fitting that in this year also, Beinn Eighe is still developing the tradition of innovative visitor facilities through a radically new Visitor Centre and trails to be centred on the building at Aultroy, where only the second Scottish National Nature Reserve Visitor Centre was opened in 1974. Highland hospitality is renowned the world over but the previous inhabitants of Aultroy could never have envisaged that so many guests might one day come to their door. These facilities have become an established part of the visitor and tourist infrastructure of Wester Ross. In today's world, where Reserve staff perforce spend more and more time in the office, the only missing element is a staff member dedicated to meeting visitors on the Trails and on the hill.

Fulfillment of aims?

It is perhaps appropriate, towards the end of this story, to look back over our shoulders to the 1940s and measure achievement against vision. First, what did these pioneers not foresee? Well, an acceptance of the public's right of access and enjoyment of Reserves and even its encouragement that developed at Beinn Eighe in the early 1960s. The fears, coincidentally expressed by private landowners at the time, that people disturbed wildlife and damaged nature conservation interests, have been totally dispelled. To an extent there never was a real threat and what pressure has arisen has been deflected by the provision of good facilities and information. Public access is now of equal importance to research and nature conservation management at Beinn Eighe, as illustrated by the latest provision of Visitor Centre and Trails.

The authors of Command 7122 hoped that Reserves would develop formal nature conservation education but this has been difficult to achieve, both because of the potential costs to the Conservancy and because of the lack of adequate funding in higher education. What they did not foresee was the incredible growth in informal education at places like Beinn Eighe, through the use of the Field Centre at Anancaun for students and volunteers. At the end of the day the lifetime experience of many may have been just as valuable as formal education.

The principal purpose of National Nature Reserves, however, was that they should be open-air laboratories, providing research opportunities for the understanding of the ecology of the countryside that would guide future management both within Reserves *and* outwith their boundaries. We hope we have demonstrated that Beinn Eighe has without doubt more than fulfilled that aim within the Reserve. Outwith, achievements are perhaps not so obvious as they are not so directly linked. But if we look we will find that the principles and policies behind woodland restoration that were established at Beinn Eighe have had a very wide influence. For example, restoration of native woodland by minimum intervention and using local provenance sources is now widespread in Scotland. It is even supported by Forestry Commission grants.

Has Beinn Eighe fulfilled the ambitious aim of influencing and benefiting the staples of the Highland economy as seen in the late 1940s? Firstly, that economy has changed out of all recognition. However, with remarkable prescience the Reserve has greatly contributed to the most important element of the Highland economy today – tourists, walkers and climbers – that hardly existed then. As far as forestry is concerned there has been an indirect influence through the creation of native woodlands by means of Forestry Commission grants. Their establishment and management provide jobs but the woodlands will take many years before they contribute timber or shelter for livestock, be it wild or domestic. As far as deer management and stalking is concerned there has been influence, but one has to say with little result. Perhaps the impetus for change in deer management will come about indirectly, from the presence of new woodlands that

Walker on the Beinn Eighe ridge.
Photo: SNH

will eventually demonstrate the benefits of fewer, larger and more productive red deer.

Lastly there is agriculture and like tourism, no one foresaw the likely changes fifty years ago. Beinn Eighe as a nature reserve has had virtually no influence here and it is hard to see how it could have, or can, through the period of restoration of its woodland. Only when that is invulnerable to grazing or browsing by domestic stock could any experiment begin and by then it might be too late. On the other hand, Beinn Eighe can demonstrate how to restore the productivity of mismanaged land, an expertise that desperately needs to be applied outwith the Reserve to the benefit of all traditional land uses.

But what about the local impact of Beinn Eighe's management? John MacKenzie of Gairloch and Conon, although critical of some aspects of Scottish Natural Heritage, has found that the attraction of the Trails and footpaths at Beinn Eighe relieves pressure on his estate where the economies of scale make it impossible for him to take advantage of visitors. Is there a great deal of difference today then between the manager of the Reserve and a private landowner as far as the local community is concerned? A recent article in the *Ross-shire Journal* suggested that: 'In contrast [to a private landowner] the manager of Beinn Eighe reserve lives locally, shops locally, attends meetings of the community council, informs locals of plans for the estate, invites local comments on management decisions and is generally available for ear-bashing!' But there needs to be more than that – and there is. The fact that Community representatives now serve on the Reserve Advisory Committee and have the opportunity to play a real part in the Reserve implies a new kind of partnership for both sides: both having to learn to balance self-interest with responsibilities to the other and to the common good.

Coille na Glas Leitir and biodiversity

A great deal of the original aims for Beinn Eighe have been achieved, and they are relatively easy to explain and demonstrate, but what of the intrinsic importance of Coille na Glas Leitir, the woodland that caught the eye of Tansley and the imagination of McVean and those who followed, and what of the connection between its protection and restoration, the rest of the Reserve and the wider environment today? This is not so easily explained.

It is a staggering truth that tropical forests hold at least half of the world's plants and animals. Our native temperate and boreal forests cannot compete with that, but nevertheless they are one of our richer habitats at this relatively high latitude and can be taken as an example of other biologically diverse native semi-natural habitats, such as wetlands, bogs, tall-herbs and mountain scrub. Today these ancient woodlands – that have a direct link back to the end of the last Ice Age – cover a mere 1 per cent of the land. That is all we have left of the once great forests of Scotland and even that tiny remnant has lost some of its species. These woodlands have taken thousands of years to evolve and cannot be recreated in all their biological complexity, at least not on a time scale that is meaningful to us.

Planting native species on ground that has long since lost its woodland results initially only in the architecture of woodland. Without mature soils beneath their trunks, the litter layers of leaves, the complex micro-habitats of fallen and rotting timber and branches, the range of plants and animals, the new woodland floor is initially almost as impoverished as surrounding moorland. Lacking too are many woodland birds and mammals, although being much more mobile they can colonise new woodland relatively quickly. What the trees and shrubs do

In the foreground new pinewood;
behind, the remnant woodland
of Allt a' Chùirn gorge and Beinn Eighe.
Photo: D. Miller

Looking out from
the high-level tall-herb enclosure.
Could the uplands be more diverse?
Photo: SNH

accomplish though, as they begin to close canopy, is to change the moorland vegetation and to control the effects of heavy rainfall by interception. The results are an improvement to soils, for the benefit of grazers, both wild and domestic, and to burns and rivers through added nutrients, reduction of temperature range and control of flash floods. To become more 'natural' – more biologically diverse – though, new woodland need secure reservoirs from which all these plants and animals can expand. Unfortunately, until very recently, most of these sources were themselves declining and many are still.

We have lost the wolf, the bear and the boar, to mention just three woodland animals, but is there still enough woodland left to sustain the pine marten and the wildcat, never mind the Scottish crossbill and never mind our distinctive woodland flora? We just do not know how large a natural system has to be to sustain its indigenous wildlife. Mentioning but a few familiar lost and declining species, among hundreds that we are hardly aware of, should remind us of just how rich and diverse our native habitats were, particularly our native woodlands. That is one reason why we should be thankful to those visionaries who saved Coille na Glas Leitir, one fragment of many, and to those who have worked so hard and long to begin to restore it across the flanks of Beinn Eighe. If this type of restoration could be applied more widely; the benefits aesthetically and economically would be immeasurable.

For example, are the natural state of Beinn Eighe's mountain heaths shrubbier and more diverse in plants, birds, mammals and invertebrates than they are and should the lime-enriched grasslands be taller and more densely adorned with flowering plants? The evidence from elsewhere in the world is an emphatic *yes*. Could it take another fifty years to understand the factors that control the health and diversity of the heath above the wood? Possibly *yes* again. It may seem that a lot has been learned about the ecology of Beinn Eighe. In fact it is only a beginning and there is still much to learn. Maybe in another fifty years other communities on Beinn Eighe will be encouraged to recover just like Coille na Glas Leitir, and maybe we will be equally astonished at the natural potential of the land once it is freed from single species management, be it deer, sheep or grouse.

Biodiversity – the diverse, unique and vastly complex assemblage of plants and animals that make up just one community or habitat, such as Coille na Glas Leitir – is one of the earth's greatest resources, important to the stability of the environment and to sustaining the human population. Much has been said elsewhere of the known importance to us all of these resources, materially and spiritually, never mind the unknown. Unfortunately, the areas we have protected by legislation and termed nature reserves, are probably not large enough in themselves to sustain all the threatened animals and plants. It is estimated that the world is losing 30,000 species a year or three an hour and we know our own contribution to this appalling fact. On an imaginary scale of naturalness, Scotland lies very much closer to England than to the 'undeveloped' countries with their relatively vast areas of natural and semi-natural habitats, such as tropical forests. However, Scotland still has large areas of semi-natural plant communities, such as those of woodland, mountain and moorland, relative to England. This is reflected in the large size of many of our Reserves. Nevertheless, many contain only a relatively tiny reservoir of those communities of animals and plants now gone from the wider countryside.

But the problem is worse than it was fifty years ago, for the world is a very different place. Development pressure on the countryside and its wildlife is very much greater and more insidious than it was, through acid rain, airborne and ground water pollution and the wide use of pesticides and inorganic fertilisers. The effect of global warming can only be guessed at, but at a minimum it will certainly result in the loss of some species at the edge of their geographical range and it may even destabilise some communities. There is also a greater public pressure on the countryside, though by and large this has been balanced by a much greater public awareness of nature conservation issues.

Diverse communities have an in-built insurance against unforeseen change, be it biological or climatological, as compared to more simple communities such as the moorland we have created through grazing and burning. They are also more productive and therefore economically more valuable. Restoration of diversity and productivity of natural systems and their sustainable management as demonstrated at Beinn Eighe, is perhaps where it can make its greatest contribution to the economy of the Highlands in the long run.

A wider perspective

By foresight and happenstance then, in 2001, Beinn Eighe National Nature Reserve is uniquely placed in regard to the new millennium issues of biodiversity, sustainability and land reform in Scotland. The Reserve is one of Britain's very few, large state-owned Reserves. It is also one that has consistently striven towards a sustainable form of management. It is now in a position to broaden its approach to sustainability and take it forward in the context of future land use in Wester Ross and in the Highlands as a whole, perhaps in partnership with others, including the local community.

In the case of Scottish Natural Heritage and Beinn Eighe this implies the involvement of and a benefit to, the local community. The former element, in a formal sense, has just begun, but the latter, especially in the form of the visitor attractions, has been in place for a number of years and has the potential for further development. The final report of the Scottish Committee in 1949 proposed that Coille na Glas Leitir should be a National Park Reserve – in other words, a Nature Reserve set within a National Park. Today, with a huge increase of visitors to the countryside, the need to co-ordinate access and recreation, to solve issues of private and public land use and to ensure local involvement and community benefits, National Parks are seen to be useful structures. Accordingly, two Scottish National Parks are in gestation: Loch Lomond and the Trossachs, and the Cairngorms.

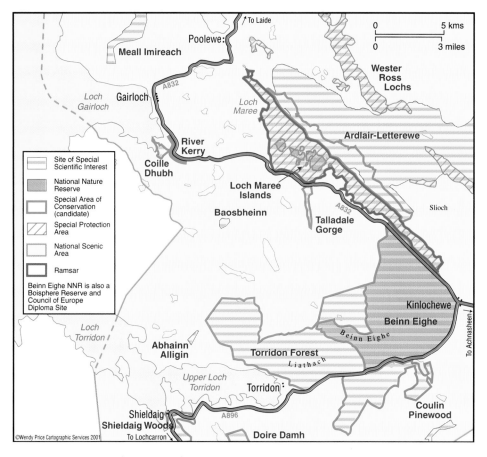

Fig 14 **Designation in the Beinn Eighe area (SSSI, NNR, NSA, prop. SAC).**

Today, Boyd's vision of co-ordinated land management in Wester Ross is more important than ever and some of the bricks of the structure are now in place. In the Beinn Eighe area we now have the National Nature Reserve managed by Scottish Natural Heritage and overlapping it The National Trust for Scotland's property of Torridon with its crofts, common grazing and crofter forestry. Both lie within the proposed Special Area of Conservation (SAC) and within the very large National Scenic Area (NSA) of Wester Ross (see Fig 14). The two bodies carry out very similar management and the former gives a great deal of financial support, through grants, to the latter. Here is where the very first bricks must be cemented together, for if co-ordinated management cannot happen here it will not happen across private estates.

Within the last decade, the introduction of the SAC has presented an opportunity for a much broader area of co-ordinated management. Beinn Eighe is within, but only a part of, the Proposed Loch Maree Complex SAC. Because this designation requires positive action to 'maintain or restore (the) natural habitats and species' of European importance it may just provide the catalyst to link management of the remnant ancient Caledonian forests of Beinn Eighe, Coulin, Torridon, the Loch Maree Islands, Talladale and maybe Shieldaig. Co-ordination of management of woodlands should not stop there, but should include the new Native Pinewood schemes that are already off the ground on estates surrounding the Reserve. It is vital also that all these woodlands are physically linked in a network to ensure successful and rapid expansion of all the indigenous plants and animals from their ancient woodland redoubts. If that principle is accepted it could be the moment to address the wider management of SAC habitats, and the Gairloch Conservation Unit has an opportunity to play a key part here.

Now that the original aims for Coille na Glas Leitir have been achieved, that monitoring of its many other habitats and species to ensure best management is in place, that its public facilities are contributing to the economy of the area and that the first local residents are sitting on its Management Advisory Group, Beinn Eighe could be said to have reached maturity: an appropriate time to seek a wider role in the world and Wester Ross in particular.

But let us leave the penultimate word on this vision for Beinn Eighe's future with Roger Crofts (SNH's Chief Executive): 'I see the Beinn Eighe Reserve continuing to live up to its original ideal and vision; a place for wildlife and earth heritage excellence, a place for research and investigation; a place for restoration of degraded land; a place for experiencing wild nature, for heightening the emotions and for learning about the environment. It is also a place for seeking the active participation of local people in its care and for visitors to enjoy and be exhilarated by, and to contribute towards, both its care and to the support of the

Beinn Eighe from across Loch Clair.
Photo: D. Miller

local community and its economy. Improving the health of the environment and its contribution to the local communities is an imperative. SNH will play its full part.'

Conclusion

We have attemped to tell the extraordinary story of the establishment of the first National Nature Reserve in Britain, the restoration of Coille na Glas Leitir and the many innovative developments in nature conservation and public involvement at Beinn Eighe, presented arguments for the conservation and expansion of areas of high biodiversity, such as that of Coille na Glas Leitir and discussed its potential influence in the wider setting of Loch Maree, Wester Ross and the Highlands. However, the most striking portrayal of the natural potential of Beinn Eighe and the Loch Maree area towards which the Reserve aspires, is actually 400 years old. It is the description given by Timothy Pont in 1600, just before the ironworks began. Part of it was quoted in our opening chapter, but here it is in full: 'The fresch loch of Ew … is 12 myl long and 4 myl broad with 24 fair yles in it … (B)etwix the salt and fresch Loch, the river runneth scars a myl, and in winter is portative for boats to bring them up to the fresch Loch, ther ar manie salmond in the river … The fair Loch is reported never to freeze. It is compasd about with many fair and tall woods as any in all the west of Scotland, in sum parts with hollyne, in sum places with fair and beautifull fyrrs of 60, 70, 80 foot of good serviceable timmer for masts and raes, in other places as great plentie of excellent oakes, whair may be sawin out planks of 4 sumtyns 5 foot broad. All thir bounds is compas'd and hemd in with many hills but thois beautifull to look on, thair skirts being all adorned with wood even to the brink of the loch for the most part'. What an extraordinarily rich environment he described, still so full of promise, but will it remain just a historical quote or could we make it a new vision?

May Beinn Eighe, Britain's first National Nature Reserve, continue to develop and innovate, and may it continue to live up to its motto: 'Air Thoiseach air Càch' (*First Among Equals*).

Postscript

Beinn Eighe was designated Britain's very first National Nature Reserve in 1951. In England the first six NNRs were Cavenham Heath, Ham Street, Holme Fen, Kingley Vale, Moor House and Yarner Wood, all declared on the same day in 1952. The first Welsh NNR was Cwm Idal, declared in 1954 and the first Nature Reserve in Northern Ireland was Bohill Wood declared in 1970. Today there are seventy-one NNRs in Scotland (presently under review), 200 in England, sixty-two in Wales and forty-six in Northern Ireland, making a grand total of 379. Scottish Natural Heritage owns 100% of the land on 17 NNRs, over 50 per cent on six and less than 50 per cent on one. The area of NNR land owned by Scottish Natural Heritage is 34,072 ha out of a total NNR area of 114,277 ha. Following the relative success of the larger, state-owned NNRs like Beinn Eighe, it is likely that any new NNRs in Scotland will be of similar size and if not owned by Scottish Natural Heritage, then owned by an approved body.

Appendix 1: enclosures

No.	area (ha.)	date est.	no. Scots pine	other	altitude (m.)	total trees
1	44	1954	4000	500 birch	13–200	4500
2 FC	125	1959		spot sowings	60–21	
3 Ex	0.5	1957	few	few whitebeam	430	
4 Div	0.8	1958–70	550	ald 182oak pop will	100	732
5 Div	0.5	1959	1170*	ald oak pop bir will row hol elm ash b.cher brm	105	170
7 Div	1	1960	1711*	460: ald oak pop bir row b.cher haz row b.cher	30	2171
8	16	1960	20,800	3270: ald oak bir	27–60	24,070
9	20	1965	59,600	9060: ald oak bir will row b.cher haz brm whin	22–115	68,660
10	18	1969	34,500	9270: ald oak bir will row b.cher haz brm whin	27–45	43,770
11	62	1971	63,000	13,495: ald oak bir will row hol b.cher haz	27–60	75,795
12	40	1975	51,000*	23,000: ald oak bir row b.cher haz brm whin	230–300	74,000
13 Dem	2	1973	1000	0	275	1000
14	40	1977	43,000*	37,300: ald oak bir row b.cher haz	150–300	80,300
15 Ex	0.5	1967	500	0	30	500
16	113	1978–99	4515	6152: ald oak bir will row hol b.cher brm asp jnp	150–300	10,662
RF	1200	1987–99	42,506	42,535: ald oak bir will row hol b.cher brm asp jnp	22–426	85,041
						467,671

FC	Forestry Commission	**ald**	alder	**brm**	broom	**pop**	poplar
Ex	Experimental	**asp**	aspen	**haz**	hazel	**row**	rowan
Div	Diversification	**b.cher**	bird cherry	**hol**	holly	**will**	willow spp
Dem	Demonstration	**bir**	birch	**jnp**	juniper		

No 2 FC 10,000 Scots pine, unknown origin; 27,000 lodgepole; 10,000 Sitka spruce.

Glen Affric provenance tree	No 5	*1170	a small number Glen Affric; all felled
	No 7	*1711	all Glen Affric; all felled
	No 12	*51,000	50,000 Glen Affric to be felled
	No 14	*43,000	34,000 Glen Affric to be felled

Appendix 2: glossary

Abhainn Cheann Loch Iù	*'the river of the head of Loch Ewe'*
Achadh na Seileach (Achnashellach)	*'the field of the willow'*
A' Chòinteach Mhòr (Coinneach Mhór)	*'the great (area of) moss'*
A' Chreag Dhubh (Creag Dhubh)	*'the black crag'*
Allt a' Chùirn	*'the burn of the cairn'*
Allt an Achaidh	*'the burn of the outfield'*
Allt an Doire Dharaich	*'the burn of the hollow of the oaks'*
Allt Bhanbhaig	*'little pig-like burn'*
Allt na h-Airbhe	*'the burn of the boundary dyke'*
Allt Sguabaig	*'little sweeping burn'*
Am Baile Mòr (Flowerdale)	*'the big (farm-)town'*
A' Mhaighdeann	*'the maiden'*
An Cnoc Gaoithe (Cnoc na Gaoithe)	*'the knoll of the wind'*
An Coire Dubh	*'the black corrie'*
An Creagan Ruadh	*'the red-brown little crag'*
An Cromfhasadh (Cromasaig)	*'the curved dwelling-place'*
An Ruadh-stac Beag	*'the smaller red steep hill'*

An Ruadh-stac Mòr	*'the greater red steep hill'*
An Sgurra Bàn (Sgurr Bàn)	*'the white peak'*
An Sleaghach (Slioch)	perhaps *'the spear-like place'*
An t-Allt Ruadh (Allt Ruadh, Aultroy)	*'the red-brown burn'*
An Teallach	*'the forge'*
An t-Sàil Mhòr	*'the great heel or spur'*
Àth nan Ceann (Anancaun)	*'the ford of the heads'*
Beinn a' Chearcaill	*'the mountain of the barrel hoop'*
Beinn Damh	*'mountain of stags'*
Beinn Eighe	*'file mountain'*
Beinn Mhòr Asainn (Ben Mór Assynt)	*'the great mountain of "Assynt"'*
Càrn Antonaidh (Carn Anthony)	*'Anthony's cairn'*
Ceann Loch Damh (Ceann Loch Damph)	*'the head of the loch of stags'*
Ceann Loch Iù (Kinlochewe)	*'the head of Loch Ewe'*
Coille na Glas-leitir (Coille na Glas Leitir, Coille na Glas-leitire)	*'the wood of the grey slope'*
Coire Mhic Fhearchair	*'the corrie of the son of Farquhar'*
Coire nan Laogh	*'the corrie of the deer calves'*

Coire Ruadh-stac	*'the corrie of the red steep hill'*
Creag Mèagaidh (Creag Meagaidh)	*'crag of the bog-place'*
Cùmhlainn (Coulin)	*'collection of enclosures'*
Frìth Cheann Loch Iù	*'Kinlochewe Deer Forest'*
Geàrrloch (Gairloch)	*'short loch'*
Gleann Dochartaidh (Glen Docherty)	*'glen of evil scouring'*
Grùididh (Grudie)	*'gravelly burn'*
Leitir Iù (Letterewe)	*'slopes of Ewe'*
Liaghach (Liathach)	*'the hoary place'*
Lochan Allt an Doire Dharaich	*'the lochs of the burn of the oak hollow'*
Loch an Tuille Bhàin	*'the loch of the white hollow'*
Loch Clàr (Loch Clair)	probably *'loch of the flat place'*
Loch Ma-Ruibhe (Loch Maree)	*'the loch of the servant of the forest or promontory'*
Meall a' Ghiuthais (Meall a' Ghiubhais)	*'the hill of the Scots pine'*
Meallan nan Cearca-fraoich	*'the little hill of the red grouse'*
Na h-Alltanan Ruadha	*'the red-brown little burns'*

Na h-Easan Dorcha	'the dark waterfalls'
Na Tathagan (Taagan)	'the small in-fields'
Poll Iù (Poolewe)	'the pool of Ewe'
Rubha 'n Fhomhair (Rhu Nòa)	'the giant's point'
Sìldeag (Shieldaig, Slattadale)	perhaps from Norse Síld-vík, 'herring bay'
Stùc Coire nan Laogh (Stùc Coire an Laoigh)	'the pinnacle of the calves' corrie'
Tealladal (Talladale)	'ledge-dale'
Toirbheartan (Torridon)	perhaps 'place of transference'
Toll a' Ghiuthais (Toll a' Ghiubhais)	'the hollow of the Scots pine'

From **Roy G. Wentworth**: *Summary of the Gaelic Place-names on Beinn Eighe National Nature Reserve* (1998).

Selected bibliography

Boyd, J. M. (1999) *The Song of the Sandpiper*. Grantown-on-Spey: Colin Baxter
    Photography.
Boyd, J. M. & Campbell, R. N. (1964) *Beinn Eighe National Nature Reserve
    Management Plan, First Revision 1965–69*. Unpublished. Nature Conservancy.
Clifford, T. (1990) *Beinn Eighe National Nature Reserve Management Plan 1990–
    94*. Unpublished. Nature Conservancy Council.
Clifford, T. & Forster, A. N. (1997) *Beinn Eighe National Nature Reserve:
    Woodland Management Policy and Practice 1944–94*. Scottish Woodland History.
    Ed. T. C. Smout.
Darling, F. F. (1955) *West Highland Survey: An Essay in Human Ecology*. Oxford:
    OUP.
Darling, F. F. and Boyd, J. M. (1964) *The Highlands and Islands*. London: Collins.
Durno, S. E. & McVean, D. N. (1959) Forest history of the Beinn Eighe National
    Nature Reserve. *New Phyt.*, 58, 228–36.
Forrest, G. I. (1980) Genotypic variation among native Scots pine populations in
    Scotland based on Monoterpene Analysis. *Forestry*, 53, No 2, 101–28.
Forster, A. N. (1993) *A review of the past management of Beinn Eighe National
    Nature Reserve, 1951–93*. SNH unpublished report.
Forster, A. (1995) *Beinn Eighe National Nature Reserve Management Plan 1995–
    2005*. Ed T. Clifford. Unpublished. Scottish Natural Heritage.
HMSO (1947) *Conservation of Nature in England and Wales*. Command Paper
    7122. London.
HMSO (1949) *Conservation of Nature in Scotland*. Command Paper 7814.
    Edinburgh.
MacGowan, I. (1994) Creating breeding sites for *Callicera rufa* and a further host
    tree.*Dipterists Digest*, 1, No 16, 8.
MacKenzie, O. H. (1922) *One Hundred Years in the Highlands*. London: ?????????
McVean, D. N. (1953) *Coille na Glas Leitir 1953 Investigations*. Reserve Record 21
    (Nature Conservancy 1953).
McVean, D. N; Arbuthnott, J. C. & Boyd, J. M. (1957) *Beinn Eighe Management
    Plan 1957*. Unpublished. Nature Conservancy
Marren, P. (1995) *The New Naturalist*. HarperCollins, London
Pearsall, W. H. (1950) *Mountains and Moorlands*. London: Collins.
Scottish Natural Heritage (1995) *Beinn Eighe Management Plan 1995–2001*.
    Unpublished. SNH, Edinburgh.
Steven, H. M. and Carlisle, A. (1959) *The Native Pinewoods of Scotland*.
    Edinburgh & London: Oliver & Boyd.
Tansley, A. G. (1939) *The British Islands and their Vegetation*. Cambridge: CUP.
Wentworth, R. G. (1998) *Summary of Gaelic Place-Names on Beinn Eighe National
    Nature Reserve*. Unpublished Report to Scottish Natural Heritage, Edinburgh.